Five Years And Two Months In The Sighet Penitentiary

(May 7, 1950 – July 5, 1955)

Five Years And Two Months In The Sighet Penitentiary

(May 7, 1950 – July 5, 1955)

by Constantin C. Giurescu

Introduction by Dinu C. Giurescu

**Edited, appendixes and index by
Lia Ioana Ciplea**

English Translation by
Mihai Farcaș and Stephanie Barton-Farcaș

EAST EUROPEAN MONOGRAPHS, BOULDER
DISTRIBUTED BY COLUMBIA UNIVERSITY PRESS, NEW YORK
1994

EAST EUROPEAN MONOGRAPHS, NO. CDVI

Copyright 1994 by Dinu C. Giurescu
ISBN 0-88033-303-0
Library of Congress Catalog Card Number 94-61340

Printed in the United States of America

TABLE OF CONTENTS

Constantin C. Giurescu
FIVE YEARS AND TWO MONTHS
IN THE SIGHET PENITENTIARY

Notes on the Edition

The book of the Romanian historian Constantin C. Giurescu brings before our eyes an upside-down world, a world that lost its landmarks, a universe ruled by arbitrary, humiliation, cruelty, fear, suspicion, and mostly by loneliness. Thus, we are faced with the whole dimension of the human abjection.

Books on the evil of the world have been written before. But what makes Professor Giurescu's testimony unique is its power to present, sine ira et studio, an era which left its marks on the destiny of contemporary humankind.

It is the book of a man who trapped in an extreme relationship – victim, executioner – took the risk of opposing life, in its whole complexity, to immoral impunity and artificial survival. Horror is converted into a lesson of morality.

In its wisdom the Talmud says: "That who saves one life saves the whole world!"

The testimony of Professor and historian Constantin C. Giurescu proves with sobriety and rigor that the one who recover History saves not only himself but also those who are to follow.

It is the exploit of a man who knows that to forget History it's a kind of immorality that might lose you.

The aim is not revenge.

Exorcising the evil asks for the power to let the Truth be known, so that no one ever could, in the name of "Good", commit the ill again.

This is the ethical legacy of the scholar Constantin C. Giurescu.

***

The testimony of his detention was kept by historian Constantin C. Giurescu in the form of a 190 page manuscript in a notebook format.

This manuscript represents the primary writing of his memoirs.

The present edition reproduces it in its entirety.

The titles of the three parts of the book – The Arrest, The Sighet Penitentiary and the Addenda – were added by me. However these titles follow naturally from the manuscript and they completely coincide with the course of events narrated by Constantin C. Giurescu. The appendixes accompanying the text were drawn up according to the express desire of historian Constantin C. Giurescu. They were completed – as much as possible – by me with a minimum of biographical data about those who suffered in Sighet penitentiary.

The three sketches are copies from the original drawings made by the author.

The English version of Appendixes belongs to Professor Dinu C. Giurescu.

The readers of today have the right to know the real dimensions of the systematic destruction of Romanian elite by the communist regime.

As main bibliographic sources I used: Ioniţoiu, Cicerone, *The Golden Book of the Romanian Resistance against Communism*, 2 vol. (vol. 1, 256 pg. & vol. 2, 211 pg.) published by the National Peasant Christian and Democratic Party; *The Royal Ministry of Foreign Affairs, Diplomatic Annual 1942*, published by the National Imprints in October of 1942; Predescu, Lucian *Cugetarea Encyclopedia – Romanian materials – People and Accomplishments*, Cugetarea, Georgescu–Delafras Publishing House, Bucharest, October 1940.

The Romanian version was published by Editura Fundaţiei Culturale Române, and was launched on March 28, 1994, Bucharest. Special thanks to scholar Zigu Ornea who supervised the printing of the Romanian version.

For the information and precision concerning the dignitaries in prison I would like to thank their descendants and friends: Pascal Bentoiu, Ioana Hudiţă Berindei, Silvia Jeleriu Ciplea, Cornelia Papacostea Danielopol, Lia Lazăr Gherasim, Bogdan Iuliu Hossu and Francine Strat Petrulian.

Also thanks to Narcisa Cimpoca, Lorita Constantinescu, Mihai Cojocea and Mihai Nasta for their technical support given with commitment and friendship.

Many heartfelt thanks to Professor Stephen Fischer-Galaţi, the publisher of the English version of Professor Constantin C. Giurescu's testimony.

My gratitude to historian Dinu C. Giurescu for having entrusted me with this edition.

Lia Ioana Ciplea

Bucharest, 1994

INTRODUCTION

1) Professor Constantin C. Giurescu was arrested in his home at 47 Berzei Street, Bucharest[1], on the morning of Saturday May 6th 1950 at the same time as the group of former state dignitaries.

At the moment of his arrest he was a scientific researcher at the History Institute of the Academy of the Romanian Popular Republic, where he had worked since July 1948, after being suspended from the History Faculty where he had been a Professor for twenty-two years.

He was transported in a police van to the prison in Sighet, where he arrived Sunday May 7th at about 6:30 in the evening. He was held in detention until July 5th, 1955 when he was notified of his "release" with a mandatory residence in the village of Măzăreni, in the district of Brăila. The village was exclusively composed of deportees from Banat who had lived there since the summer of 1951. In November 1955 the Professor was given "approval" to return to Bucharest, to his family. He left Măzăreni on November 25th.

The "approval" was given by the Ministry of the Interior due to the intervention of Dr. Petre Groza, president of the Presidium of the Great National Assembly, at the request of Professor Giurescu's family.

Lawyer Adrian Brudariu had been very helpful in getting the release.

In the village of Măzăreni, twelve days after notification of his

---

[1] The house, a villa with a semi-basement, two floors and an attic, was built by my parents – Constantin C. Giurescu and Maria Simona Giurescu (Mica, daughter of Simion S. Mehedinți and Maria Mehedinți) – between 1926 and 1929, with a loan from the Teachers's Corp of Bucharest. The new building included a part of the house bought by my grandfather, Constantin Giurescu, at the beginning of the century.

The Giurescu house was nationalized in April 1950, although it wasn't the object of any of the articles of law pertaining to nationalization of buildings.

In December 1973, the apartment on the first floor of the villa was returned to Professor Constantin C. Giurescu; the other parts of the building remained the property of the State. The house was torn down in August 1987, when the entire zone between Berzei Street (in the east), Știrbei Vodă Street (in the south), Calea Plevnei (in the west) and Virgiliu Street (in the north) was demolished as part of "urban systematization" ordered by the communist regime.

release (July 17, 1955), Constantin C. Giurescu began to compile notes about his time in Sighet. He completed an abbreviated version of this work on November 12th. His intention to extend these notes is shown by the numerous facts that he briefly mentions in the "Addenda" (pages 111-124)[2]. He did not continue this work, and was soon hired as a part time researcher at the History Institute of the Academy of the Popular Republic of Romania.

In 1958 the communist regime proceeded to make new arrests and conduct new trials, "unmasking" in public meetings all intellectuals accused of deviating from the party line. At that time we talked about the "notes" in the family, because their discovery would have led automatically to the author's arrest and conviction. Constantin C. Giurescu entrusted the manuscript to a good friend, lawyer Nicolae (Nicu) Ionescu-Caracaleanu, and his former cabinet director (between 1939-40). During the fascist rebellion on January 21-23, 1941, lawyer Nicolae Caracaleanu together with his brother Grigore Ionescu stayed in the house on Berzei Street together with my parents, and had loaded hunting rifles, in case the "rebels" tried to enter the house.

The Sighet Manuscript was buried by lawyer Nicolae (Nicu) Caracaleanu in his parents' houses' garden, situated on Calea Călărași, not far from the intersection with Traian Street.

After the Professors' death (November 13, 1975), lawyer Caracaleanu brought the manuscript back to me at my request. In the 80's I thought it was better for me to protect the "notes". At present they are kept by Professor Paul Michelson's library (Huntington College, Huntington, Indiana).

After my arrival with my family in the United States (April 12, 1988), Professor Paul Michelson sent me a photocopy of the manuscript. The present edition is based on this photocopy.

***

2) Professor Constantin C. Giurescu's notes are a document on the Sighet Penitentiary where, between 1950-55, over one hundred leaders of the political, religious and cultural life were imprisoned. "It is a simple testimony which will be used by future historians". It

---

[2] All references in parentheses refer to this edition

includes the authors' own experience and facts he learned from others.

The first part – "The Arrest" presents chronologically: the secret police's "visit" to 47 Berzei Street, the wait at the Ministry of the Interior, the journey to Sighet -the only description, as far as I know, of the transportation of this group to detention.

The second part – "The Sighet Penitentiary" describes multiple components and aspects of the communist prison, a mechanism of breaking people: the imprisonment itself; the "adjustment" to the new environment; the detailed description of the building, with three blueprints drawn by the author; the staff of the prison – director, assistant director, duty officers, wardens, and secret police officers; aspects of daily life: "Neagra" (the Black Cell), cleaning of the common spaces, the "conferences" held by the prisoners...

The third part – "Addenda" includes additional information and details. Most of them describe, in a few words, tragic happenings.

The appendices were completed by Mrs. Lia Ioana Ciplea according to the authors' specifications. Some of the realities in this testimony need to be stressed.

"The system[3], especially during the first three years, was bestial..."

The "daily" life was permanently dominated by suspicion and fear: "the mistrust of everyone for each other, spying on each other, these were the basic principles in the relationship among the prison's staff. There was an atmosphere of terror not only for the prisoners, but also for the wardens. 'Here in prison is the biggest infamy' warden Gavrilă Pop from Vișeul de Sus told me one evening in January 1951 when he brought firewood for me, 'We all shiver, not only you, but we too.'" (The wardens, page 73). The fear and suspicion were actually multiplying the reality of the communist world outside.

As everywhere, the basic rule forbade all communication between prisoners. The rule was circumvented by the prisoners' ingenuity.

In June 1955, when a 'détente' was beginning in the outside world[4], new restrictive rules were introduced: in the cells the prisoners were permitted to talk only in a low voice and only between two people, they were not allowed to hold 'conferences' with the others;

---

[3] The communist system – *DCG note*

[4] The meeting between U.S. president Dwight Eisenhower and Nichita S. Hrusciov took place in July 1955 in Geneva

they would face the wall when a staff member came in; they would all sleep with their heads in the same direction so that the warden could see their faces when he looked through the observation opening; they would keep their hands in sight, above the blanket.

The general regime in the prison was suggestively described by the director of the penitentiary: "We, the communists, do not kill, we have our methods to bring you to despair." (page 62). Professor Giurescu's comment follows: "What he said was true about Sighet: the prisoners killed themselves out of despair, they perished because of diseases and lack of medical care, they became insane. I believe there is no other prison in the country which had such a large percentage of deaths, suicides and insanity.".

The hatred for prisoners was fed by "regular meetings on Saturday and Wednesday. Meetings in which all kind of lies and slander were produced...It was a systematic action of continual embittering of the staff; in these meetings we were presented as 'vampires' who 'sucked the people's blood' , 'bestial land-owners', 'exploiters of the proletariat', bad guys who used to have 'parties and orgies with champagne' and other things of this nature".

From his very first days of detention on May 13, 1950, the Professor heard one of the wardens screaming at one of the prisoners upstairs: "So what if you were a general? You're nothing now! Move faster when I tell you, otherwise I will slap your eyes out of your head, damn you, son of a bitch!" (page 38)

The communists' goal was to imprint with tenacity in the wardens' mind of, "contempt for what was the leading class in the past; this class was the symbol of sin, incompetence and dishonesty, in contrast, of course with the present leading class (the communist class), which concentrates all virtues and knowledge" (page 73)[5].

During the first three years of prison time the food was reduced to the minimum: two hundred and fifty grams of bread (in reality only two hundred and twenty or thirty) for twenty four hours; in the morning a sort of water with a vague smell of lime instead of tea. "From May 8, 1950 to July 3, 1953 barley was the main meal in prison, and there were periods, like between December 20, 1950 and

---

[5] The same spirit, of hatred and contempt for those who were somebody or had something in the past was repeatedly cultivated, to the point of hysteria, by mass-media and the communist literature between 1948-60 (D.C.G.).

January 5, 1951[6] when we were given it all the time for lunch and dinner" (page 33). The "dinner" consisted of "barley soup, in reality a sort of leftover dish water".

The sensation of hunger becomes permanent. "A half an hour after you finish your lunch, you are hungry again; this sensation becomes more and more intense and grows to its fullest at half past five in the evening when, usually, the bell for dinner rings. After the watery soup in the evening you don't even have a half an hour respite like with lunch; you are hungry the moment you finish eating" (page 40). Only in the second half of 1953 was there a certain improvement of the meals.

The prisoners were forced to perform all kinds of work: chop wood, carry the tubs of food, wash the floor, carry the containers of feces to the toilet, clean the latrines and empty them of feces.

The toilet was "a hole cut in the dirty cement of the floor. Water was nonexistent...." (page 29)

In most of the toilets there was no proper drainage of liquids into the hole, "So in the morning after emptying and cleaning the containers of feces and taking water in the mess tins, we would find the floor covered with 1–2 centimeter layer of liquid [7]; we had to take this liquid with a dustpan or with rags, and put it into the holes..." (page 56)

Cleaning of the toilets was done by prisoners, "With hands in urine, using rags." Boca, one of the wardens, "took a real sadistic pleasure in making us clean the toilets."

They did the same thing with the sewers which were clogged periodically. "Dumitru Nistor[8] was forced to get into the sewer and take out the filth [9] with buckets that his cell-mates carried further; when he came out of the sewer he had filth all over his body." (page 101)

The wardens, some of them real beasts, were known by the initial 'B' – for beast – namely B-1, B-2, B-3, B-4...others were only "curs" – C-1, C-2. With a few exceptions, the real name of the wardens was unknown to the prisoners.

---

[6] This period coincides with the winter holidays

[7] in fact it was urine

[8] Deputy State Secretary during the Sănătescu government

[9] the fecal matter

B-1 was also called "the Mongoloid": "he stunk so bad that you felt ill around him"; he always cursed. Arba, formerly imprisoned for murder, "cursed like B-1 and had taken a sadistic pleasure in tormenting and humiliating the prisoners". "Pithecanthropus erectus" was "one of the most bestial wardens...if not the most bestial" of all the wardens of Sighet. "a serious alcoholic, with the face of a degenerate, growling rather than speaking..."; greedy, he stole from the meager food of the prisoners (page 84).

But there were also wardens who, despite the existing regime, managed to remain human, and help the prisoners as far as they could, by carrying messages, by giving words of encouragement, by giving extra food...among these, we need to mention "the Aviator", Gavrilă Pop, "the Barber", "Cireşică" (Little Cherry). Their words and gestures meant, of course, something to the people plunged into suffering, misery and intolerance.

For the smallest infringement of the by-laws – sometimes a wardens' or officers' fantasy – additional penalties were applied in "Neagra" – a cell without windows. Those who were punished were put in wearing only a shirt and underwear or even completely naked. Other times you were forced to spend a half an hour in the 'bustard' position – squatted with the hands outstretched horizontally; not allowed to lean on anything for support: after about fifteen minutes this position became really painful.

The world of the Sighet prison – like all the other prisons in the country – directly reflected some features of the communist regime. These were defined as follows by Constantin Giurescu:
– "mistrust, mutual spying and informing" (page 18)
– "suspicion and mutual fear...two of the fundamental principles of the regime" (the communist regime) (page 37)
– "simulation...another feature of the system: people say things that they don't believe, they express opinions and feelings that they don't have and that in their soul they contest and even despise" (page 81)

* * *

3) Professor Constantin C. Giurescu knew himself all the "procedures" and measures applied in Sighet.

He was kept isolated in a cell from May 7, 1950 to January 25, 1952. In order to not lose track of the days he scratched, in the door's thick paint, one mark every day, beginning with May 7, 1950. For Sundays the mark was longer and notched to the left; the days when a special event happened or he received news were also marked with a longer line notched to the right. In order to compensate for the pressure of isolation, the Professor used to tackle and re-tackle in his mind a series of research topics, to check his vocabulary in foreign languages, and to draft the plan and the components of a new work.

In the first days he couldn't eat although at that time the food was a little more consistent compared with what was to follow. "Why didn't you finish your beans[10]?" the warden asked him. "Because I cannot!" "That's not good... later you will be so hungry that you will chew on the walls" (page 32)

When he was given his prison uniform instead of civilian clothes, the pants were too tight in the waist and he couldn't button the two upper buttons: "don't worry, they will fit you in two weeks; they will be just right", the director said (page 39). So it was; in two weeks the trousers fit him and two months later they were too big.

He became so thin that the Greek Catholic Bishops and Priests who were in the yard, didn't recognize him when he appeared at the cell windo.

When he was alone in cell number twenty-one, one evening at midnight, he was beaten by four wardens, among them one who was nicknamed 'Nasone'.

Constantin C. Giurescu was put in "Neagra" eight times (page 98).

In June of 1950, during the "first outbreak of hatred and aggression, when the penalties were coming one on top of another, when the 'Neagra' was functioning all the time", the Professor got up on the bed in order to look at the prisoners in the yard, but he got off before the warden 'Arba' unexpectedly entered the cell. This man asked the Professor three times whether he wanted to look out the window, promising that he wouldn't punish him if he answered truthfully. The Professor had the naiveté to confess. For only having the intention to look out the window he was put in 'Neagra'.

One month after his arrival in Sighet, warden 'Boca' accused him of having made a puddle of urine in the toilet when he emptied the

---

[10] mashed beans

container of feces. The following "dialogue" took place:

Boca (B): You made a puddle on the floor; I will make you lick it up.

CCG: I didn't spill a drop.

B: Yes you did, I saw you.

CCG: You didn't see anything, because at the moment you appeared at the door I had finished and was rinsing the container.

B: Clean the floor immediately; I want to see the moon and the bulb shine on the floor, otherwise you're in trouble.

CCG: I have nothing to clean with.

B: (shrieking) with your cap!

CCG: I won't do it with my cap...

B: Then do it with this (he throws a hand sized rag)

The Professor cleaned everything, because a refusal to obey the wardens' order was considered "a serious infraction".

The dialogue continued:

Boca: It's not good, wipe the liquid[11] again.

CCG: There's nothing left, I wiped up all the liquid.

B: Shut up and wipe; otherwise I will make you scrub it until evening.

CCG: I will report this mockery to the director.

B: You can report; which one of us do you think he'll believe? It's still me whom he'll believe; scrub and don't say a word, you son of a bitch.

CCG: I will report you for cursing too.

B: (after five minutes) Get your ass to your cell.

Another time, when he was on kitchen duty, he and the others were made to wash the floor three times. In 1954, on St. Constantin and Elena's day (May 21st), when it was his name day, the Professor participated in carrying the buckets of feces taken from the sewers that were clogged again.

He was ill twice. In spring of 1951 he had "a rather serious kind" of "jaundice" which lasted three months. He was left only skin and bones. Yellow as if he was "dyed with saffron", he was brought to the big yard one afternoon, watched by a soldier. Warden 'Arba' came and said "You know you can die of this disease?" (page 76)

CCG: "Thank you for your encouragement".

---

[11] in fact urine

Arba: "I didn't say it on purpose to you, but you know you can die of it".

After Arba walked away the soldier who was watching said something under his breath: "He's a mother-fucking bastard".

Another warden, "the Barber" had encouraging words for him. Twice he brought the Professor some rubbing alcohol: "This is good for you", he said; "don't tell anybody that I gave you this" (page 88)

The second time he suffered again from jaundice in the autumn of 1954. He was taken out of the "community" of cell number 18 and moved alone to cell 60 (October 13). "I was close to death," remembers the Professor later in Măzăreni in 1955. "What kept me alive was only the will to live, to get out and be with all of you again". He said once in Sighet that even if only a few of them would stay alive there he would be among them. The will to live and the faith in his work kept him whole. On the day of his imprisonment, May 7, 1950, an officer asked him: "Are you the author of the History of Romanians?" After he answered yes, the officer added: "Nowadays the history of Romania is written differently". The Professor responded: "It's possible, but our history remains only one history."

He went through this new hardship. On February 7, 1955 he returned to the "community" of cell number 18 (see the chronology of his detention). While he had been isolated in cell 60 "Bălăcescu", "one of the nicest wardens" came daily to check on his health, and asked him in the morning if he didn't want extra food.

By the middle of June 1955 – about three weeks before his "release" – the new director of the hospital called him a "bandit". The director was dissatisfied because he couldn't prove a false allegation about the Professor and Aurelian Bentoiu.

* * *

4) I found out about my fathers' arrest on Saturday, May 6, 1950 when I came home from the village Andrășești (Ialomița County). I was sent there as a road construction foreman with a company "SOVROM – Constructions Number 6" (its' headquarters were on Calea Dorobanți number 14, in the house of the former head of the National Liberal Party, Constantin I. C. Brătianu, himself imprisoned in Sighet). I was welcomed at the door by my uncle, Emil S.

Mehedinți, who told me the news and added that other former dignitaries were arrested in the same night.

The only information about the Professors' fate I received in 1954 (I don't remember which month). I was living with my mother in one room in the parish house of the Mavrogheni Church (Monetăriei Street number 4), where we received the hospitality of Father Grigore Burlușanu and his family[12.] One morning we received a visit from historian Zenovie Pâclișanu who told us that my father was in Sighet in 1951 and that he was ill but had recovered; he did not have more recent information.

As for the rest, we heard only rumors that circulated during the first months of 1955 when international "relaxation" began to be mentioned.

I saw the Professor again on the first Sunday after July 5, 1955 in the deportees' village Măzăreni (Brăila County) where I arrived in the morning with my mother and my sister, Simona.

Constantin C. Giurescu had been assigned to the peasant Vasile Pigulea, himself deported in 1951 from Banat. The house, made of mud bricks, had only one room and an entrance hall where there was a stove on which they cooked food. There in the entrance hall they installed a bed made of planks on which the Professor and my mother slept. My mother spent a long time in Măzăreni between July and November of 1955.

When I saw him again, after sixty-two months of "absence", I couldn't recognize him at first. At that time he was fifty-three years and eight months old. He had lost almost all his teeth. His face was emaciated, with very pronounced features. When he began to smile I realized that he was my father. "Well, I look well now", he told us, "you should have seen me in 1952 or when I came out of my last jaundice crisis!".

After the arrests in May of 1950 the communist regime adopted harsh measures against families too.

We continued to live in the house on Berzei Street 47 until the last days of June 1950: my mother – Maria-Simona Giurescu (Mica, daughter of Simion and Maria S. Mehedinți) ; my sister – Simona Giurescu – student in philology; Dinu C. Giurescu; the grandparents:

---

[12] with their daughter Dr. Cornelia (Nely) Butănescu, their son-in-law Dr. Mihai Butănescu and their granddaughter Mihaela (Moața)

Simion S. Mehedinți[13] and Maria Mehedinți. Also, Emil S. Mehedinți, lawyer and ex-industrialist[14], used to often sleep in our house. In 1950 he was working as a land surveyor, in a group belonging to the Bucharest Town Hall.

In May 1950 (after professor's arrest) Dr. Gh. (Gică) Mănescu and his wife Sanda moved into our house. They were evacuated together with the family of Dr. Titel Vereanu[15] from the house on Făgăraș Street, the house having been requisitioned by the authorities. Such expulsions became frequent in 1949-50. (The villa is still on Făgăraș Street. It escaped demolition in August and September of 1985, because it housed the Mongolian Embassy.)

This was the way we lived for a few weeks. We also had heard a rumor saying that very soon those who were arrested would be sorted out and the Professor could be released!

On one of the last days of June – soon after the Korean War broke out, I heard the doorbell ringing repeatedly and persistently. It was morning, before 7:00. I went down the stairs from my room on the second floor and saw several silhouettes through the frosted glass window of the door. I opened the peephole and saw two policemen and two civilians: "Is the Giurescu family living here?" "Yes!" "We have an evacuation order. You move to Alexander Moruzi Street number... the move will be done immediately!" "What do you mean by immediately? Do we have to pack?" "Yes, you are allowed to take strictly personal effects and a mattress each!" All four entered and scattered in the house on the first and second floor.

My mother fainted, but she soon recovered. She recognized the man who led the group. It was Comrade Weber from the Living Space Administration who was dealing with evacuations of houses and apartments. He was short and thin, with a sallow complexion. A short time earlier he had evacuated the family of engineer Luca

---

[13] The founder of the chair of Geography at Bucharest University, member of the Romanian Academy, expelled from it when it was re-organized under the name of the Academy of Romanian Popular Republic in 1948; the house Mehedinți – Dimitrie Rakoviță Street number 12 – was requisitioned and emptied by autumn of 1944.

[14] He organized and developed the fabric mill in Balotești (Ilfov). The factory was nationalized in June 1948.

[15] Dr. Titel Vereanu and his wife Suzi, good friends of my parents.

Bădescu, his wife Lelia[16] and their daughters, Ruxandra and Măriuca from their house on Aviators' Boulevard. My mother helped them to pack their things, and on this occasion she met comrade Weber. A family with higher connections within the communist party had moved immediately into the Bădescu house (next to the Parhon Hospital). In the rush to leave the house we had wanted to take some of the Professors' suits. "He doesn't need them any more, don't take anything." we were told. I wanted to keep a wristwatch that had belonged to my father but they took it away from me. They almost tore the earrings out of my mothers' and sisters' ears.

At about 11:00 a.m. we were put into a truck, with two suitcases and a mattress each and moved to Alexandru Moruzi Street, to the specified address: two rooms, one with a wooden floor, the other with a dirt floor; one of them had a bulb in the ceiling. There was no bathroom. No kitchen. The toilet was in the yard. This space was reserved for the families Giurescu – 3 persons, and Mehedinți – 2 persons.

All the belongings in the house on Berzei Street 47 were confiscated. No inventory was done and we received no receipt. My fathers' library, spanning two generations – at least two thousand volumes – was pillaged.

In those days, my mother visited Professor Mihail Ralea and Professor Petre Constantinescu-Iași, and pleaded with them to save the library, by arranging for it to be taken over by the History Institute of the Academy. The former, in a polite tone of voice, and the latter in a rude and sharp tone, responded that they could not do anything[17]. Thousands of pages of notes, original documents and correspondence were gathered and burned later in the yard in front of the house. The new regime of popular democracy didn't need the values belonging to the "enemies". Paintings – Grigorescu, Petrașcu, Tonitza – disappeared without a trace. They couldn't be found later in any museum![18] Also all the carpets, Romanian rugs, furniture – including

---

[16] The Professor Constantin C. Giurescu's sister.

[17] We recovered however about two hundred to two hundred and fifty volumes and reviews in 1956 from the History Institute where they were stored, but nobody knows who stored them or when.

[18] Two paintings – 'Peasant Woman' by Nicolae Grigorescu and 'Bell Tower' by Nicolae Petrașcu, escaped the looting thanks to Dr. Gică Mănescu and Sanda Mănescu. These paintings were in the double room occupied by them. When they

my parents' bedroom set made of cherry wood – disappeared. Also gone were the bookcases made of oak wood that covered three walls of the Professors' study. We lost a Romanian stamp collection comprised of all the issues starting with Alexandru Ion Cuza's reign in 1859 up until 1955. In addition to this we lost all the current inventory of the house – dishes, silverware, clothes, two radios and records – everything we had accumulated over twenty-one years.

The looting was total and the individual beneficiaries of it remained unknown. I learned at the time about similar measures adopted against the families of those others arrested on May 6, 1950. Later, in 1956, the government issued a decision that legalized, retrospectively, the looting of June 1950.

In fact, the history of the communist regime in Romania is the history of successive expropriations applied on a national scale. They started in 1945 and continued until December 1989. In the 80's when everything seemed to be taken by the socialist state, the last expropriations began – a demolition of the houses in towns and the flattening of villages, the imposing of prices upon agriculturists that were much lower than the real market prices value of produce and the virtual confiscation of surpluses of collective farms through compulsory sellings to the state at fixed prices. In addition one has to mention the expropriations forced upon consumers, by depriving them of the food necessary for a minimum of normalcy.

The wanderings of the Giurescu family continued. Being an "employee" at a building site, I was "given" a new place to live. We were received by the lawyer Petre Ghițulescu and his wife Aretie[19] in the apartment they occupied on Domnița Anastasia Street, not far from where it intersected with Brezoianu Street. They had the courage and kindness to give us a room although they knew the position we were in. We lived here until the middle of September when I received a phone call at the building site (I was working in Alexeni, Ialomița County, not far from Urziceni), telling me that my mother and my sister had been evacuated by the same comrade Weber. This man was screaming that he was going to slap me for having dared to leave the "home" that was given to us at the end of

---

were moved to a new address they took the paintings with them and gave them back to us when the professor was released.

[19] I was a friend of their sons, Bebe and Radu.

June. Eventually we ended up at Alexandru Ciurcu street (not far from Crucea de Piatră Street which was known for its' brothels – already closed in 1950). We were "given" a room with a hall at the far end of a yard, with a water supply and an outside toilet. The Ghițulescu family were punished for their gesture. The room we had lived in was confiscated. With difficulty, over time, by successive moves they managed to leave the apartment and to find another.

During the winter of 1950-51 we benefited from the repeated hospitality of my uncle's ex-wife, Wanda Mehedinți (born Branicki) who, together with her children Șerban and Mona (my first cousins) and her son-in-law, Dr. Traian Ștefănescu, occupied three rooms in their former house on Ștefan Mihăilianu Street. Our visits to them meant for us, aside from moral support, the possibility of taking a warm bath.

In the summer of 1951 we managed to move – this time with "approval" – into a room at the Parish house of the St. Maria Church (behind the St. Vineri cemetery). The house was situated on the Carol Knappe dead-end street (formerly N. Șerban Street). Here we benefited from the kind lodging of Parish Father Șerbănescu and his wife.

In the autumn of 1953 we moved again – with the approval of the patriarchy – into the Parish house of the Mavrogheni Church, on Monetăriei Street number 4 (near Piața Victoriei), where my grandparents Simion and Maria S. Mehedinți were living. Here we were constantly supported by Father Grigore Burlușanu and here too – into the same room – the Professor returned in November 1955. In this way we benefited twice from the direct help of the Church.

During these years, my mother made necklaces and other ornaments and this helped her make some money. Out of my wage of 1,200 lei monthly[20] I used to give her at least half. Whenever I came home from the building site I enjoyed her care and a "home-cooked" meal. She never complained about our situation but she faced it calmly.

My sister Simona began to work in a installation plant in June 1950. She did the work naturally as if she had worked there forever. Later she got married; life went on. Whenever I came to Bucharest I had moments of leisure and relaxation at her home.

The second son in our family, Dan, was in Paris from December

---

[20] Basic salary plus 'on-site' allowance

1946 on. He was given, for the first year, a scholarship from the French government. Obviously gifted in mathematics and having a real talent for painting and drawing he began to study architecture and worked at the same time in order to support himself. We used to get letters from him before and after 1950. We kept him informed of our address. He found out, there in Paris, about our fathers' arrest, but he never asked us about it because that would have had unpleasant consequences for us here... When he learned about the Professor's return he sent us a telegram saying that this was one of the happiest days of his life.

Lieutenant-Colonel Horia Alexandru Giurescu (1904 – 1994), the brother of Professor Constantin C. Giurescu, was imprisoned between 1951 – 1956. He went through all the rigors of the communist prisons.

Vasile Antonescu, Senator of the Liberal Party, brother of Elena Giurescu (the wife of Constantin Giurescu, my paternal grandfather), was also arrested and he died in prison in 1952.

* * *

5) Constantin C. Giurescu resumed his work as early as July 1955. On the second Sunday after his release, I asked him: "Well what are we going to do now?" he responded promptly: "We start to work!"

He asked me to bring him back issues of literature during the time of his imprisonment. I bought him the volumes *Documente privind istoria României (Documents Concerning the History of Romania)* that he read and annotated one by one.

After he was hired as a part time researcher by the History Institute of the Academy, he prepared (1956) and published (1957), with the help of Mircea Ionescu-Voicana, editor in chief at "Scientific Publishing House", the volume *Principatele Române la începutul secolului XIX. Constatări istorice, economice și statistice pe temeiul hărții ruse din 1835 (The Romanian Principalities at the Beginning of the 19th Century. Historical, Economic and Statistical data based on the Russian Map of 1835)*, 318 pages plus two pages of illustrations. The entire volume was of new research that came ten years after his previous printed work (in 1947). This first volume caused an adverse reaction and only in 1964 was he able to publish a second book, although the monograph *Istoria Bucureștilor*

(The History of Bucharest) had been given to the publisher, as early as 1958.[21]

This second stage in the scientific and didactic (begun in 1964) activity of Professor Constantin C. Giurescu ended on November 13, 1977[22]. This stage is as important as the first one (1919-1947), because of the variety and novelty of the subjects, because of their analysis, because of the new ideas put forth and the new perspectives.

***

The Sighet Penitentiary, as well as all of the communist prisons and camps, were mechanisms devised to break people and destinies and make outcasts of the survivors. There are not many exceptions to this.

I asked the Professor how he could withstand this mechanism and how he managed to come back into the mainstream of the scientific community. The prevalent things – the Professor told me at the time, in 1955-56, and later again – were:

– The will to survive, to withstand in any situation the repeated attempts of the wardens;

– The safeguarding of psychological and intellectual integrity by continuing his own mental work while in prison, using only his memory and exercising it continually any (the possession of a pencil or paper was punishable the same as infraction of rules);

– The determination to recover the time wasted in prison, at the same time as the strict keeping of the daily work schedule;

– The passion for his profession, which gave great guidance to his life; the active interest in new research topics and areas;

– The persistence in surmounting numerous obstacles raised by those having the communist regime mentality (for example, the "technique" of ad hoc reviews used to prevent the publishing of a work).

---

[21] La bibliographie des oeuvres du professeur Constantin C. Giurescu, in Revue Roumaine d'Histoire, t. XI, no. 3, 1972, pg. 547-563 and t. XVI, no. 2, pg. 373-379, Bucharest, 1977. In 1948-49 he had already elaborated on a part of "Istoria Românilor în Secolul al XIX-lea" (The History of Romanians in the 19th Century), a continuation of the five volumes issued by Royal Foundations Publishers, 1935-47. I couldn't find the manuscript again.

[22] This is the day when Constantin C. Giurescu he passed away.

Thus, step by step, the personality and the work of Professor Constantin C. Giurescu imposed themselves on the political forums in the 60's and 70's.

And the communist regime, in its' own interest, allowed – within the known limits – the scientific, scholastic and literary activities of the prominent personalities of the 30's and 40's.[23]

6) After the events of December of 1989, the realities of the communist prisons and camps began to be, with difficulty, known. There is a diversity of testimonies. Some of them are chronicles of events; others tend to be literary accounts; some stress emotional elements; some of them manage to present facts detachedly.

Whatever their character is, these accounts unveil a reality that many people still refuse to acknowledge; some people deny it. Others even mock it or they disrespect the suffering of hundreds of thousands of people who collectively spent millions of years in prison.

After 1989 some peoples' infamy turned out to be as great as that of the tormentors in the years 1946-60.

The generation that today is around the age of fifty does not know the true face of the communist regime between 1945 and the

---

[23] By the beginning of the 60's, the communist regime realized that it needed the scholars who began their work in the 30's. Within the ideological limits (although in attenuated variants compared with the 40's and the 50's), Constantin C. Giurescu did research and published on a diversity of subjects: The History of Fishing...(389 pages, 1964); The Life and Deeds of Cuza Vodă (469 pages, 2 editions – 1966 and 1970); Information about the Romanian Population of Dobrogea in the Medieval and Modern Maps (64 pages, 1966); The History of Bucharest...(465 pages, 1967); The History of the town of Brăila (373 pages, 1968); The History of the Odobești Vineyard (with 124 unpublished documents, 551 pages, 1968); Travel Journal (in U.S.A., England, France, 269 pages, 1971); Contributions to the Study of the Origin and Development of the Romanian Bourgeoisie before 1848 (296 pages, 1972); Contributions to the History of the Romanian Science and Technique between the 15th Century and the Beginning of the 19th Century (268 pages, 1973); The Formation of the Romanian People (173 pages, 1973); The History of the Romanian Forest (388 pages, 1975); Memories (340 pages, 1976); Controversial Problems in the Romanian Historiography (176 pages, 1977). In addition to this are The History of Romanians (Compendium 830 pages, 1971, 2nd edition in 1975) and The History of Romanians volumes I and II (340 pages, 1974 and 448 pages, 1976). These three works were published in collaboration with Dinu C. Giurescu. Constantin C. Giurescu published also over one hundred articles and studies.

beginning of the 60's. The explanation for this is rather simple. It was given to me by the Romanian Prime Minister in October 1992 when I met him at a reception. Our parents – the Prime Minister said – did not tell us about the hardship they went through or heard about in the 40's and the 50's. We – their children – went to college at the beginning of the 60's, when the communist regime had changed its methods, it was looking for public support and had started opening to the West. After we graduated, each of us started his own job, having to face the specific realities of the 70's and 80's. Thus, the true face of things in the first twenty years of the communist regime remained unknown or somehow unclear, almost without an outline.

Of course, the memories about the prisons unveil one side of the former regime. But what about the other sides?

During the last three years, many institutions and publications adopted a policy of ignoring, hiding and forgetting. Very little, much too little, is said about the tragedies during the collectivization, about the systematic expropriation of the peasant class and any other small producers including the artisans with their own workshops. Very little is said about the destruction of the normal economic mechanisms and their replacement with planned quotas and ruling by the party and state bureaucracy.

In the 80's, after over thirty years of communist regime, an entire country worked for the survival of the "socialist industry". This was an industry initiated and continued upon the basis of ideological priorities and obsessions. It was continually developed, without any care for the needs and the resources of the country. This industry, in the 80's, was consuming the water, heat, electricity, food and medical care necessary for a decent.

All these realities of the former regime are being hidden or ignored in many forums and by important sections of the mass media.

Numerous discussions during the last three years did not attack the main problem: how much and what remains of the widely heralded socialist industry.

Under the pressure of the hard present conditions they have to face, too few people realize that today's hardship is primarily a result of the communist regime.

What we need is not the trial of communism but the knowledge of communism.

Getting to know it, revealing its' mechanisms, methods and especially its' consequences, everyone can understand the way one should react and contribute to the return to a normal life.

A return which requires the necessary will to get away from evil and move towards good.

The testimony of Professor Constantin C. Giurescu could now be a support and an impulse to do that.

Dinu C. Giurescu
January 10, 1993
Bucharest, Romania

FOREWORD

I present a document about what happened in Sighet: what I saw with my own eyes or what I learned from other people who also saw things with their own eyes.

Thus, this is a book of memoirs.

I wrote it immediately after my release from prison; I began it on July 17, 1955 in Măzăreni where I had a mandatory domicile and I continued it until November 12, 1955; on November 25, 1955 I moved to Bucharest.

For some of the information I am obliged to my friends and fellow sufferers: Aurelian Bentoiu, Nicolae Cornățeanu, Victor Papacostea, Romulus Pop, Nicolae Sibiceanu, and others.

The book is dedicated to the memory of the over sixty fellows who rest eternally in Sighet on the shore of the Iza river.

I wrote this book "with no hatred or partiality". I tried to depict things *as they were in reality*. I did not have in view either literary or political ends. It is a simple testimony which will be used by future historians.

For some of the facts, other testimonies will of course be produced, giving commentaries about the contents of this book. Based on all these accounts, tomorrow's historian will be able to write the history of the years of suffering in Sighet, where we escaped none of the moral sufferings and torments.

Constantin C. Giurescu

To the memory of those who rest eternally on the shores of the Iza river.

Constantin C. Giurescu

THE ARREST

The arrival of the secret police

Saturday May 6, 1950, four o'clock in the morning.

The front doorbell rings constantly and persistently. We awake suddenly; my wife goes to the hall and asks: "Who is it?" I don't hear the answer, but in a few moments she re-enters the bedroom and, her face stricken with fear, she whispers to me, enunciating the syllables, "Se-cu-ri-ta-tea!" (Secret Police). I take her hand and say: "Stay calm, I'm going to see what they want." I put my working clothes on and I go to the hall and crack the front door. In front of me there is an individual about forty years old, with a tired face – it's obvious he didn't sleep at all the night before – who holds in his hand three sheets of printed paper. He asks me: "Is Professor Giurescu living here?" and at the same time, he sticks the point of his shoe between the door and the doorjamb, so that I cannot close it. After my affirmative answer, he asks me again: "Where is he?" "I'm he." he inspects me – I can see he expected me to be older – he looks again at his papers and insists: "Are you sure it's you?" "Yes, it's me; what do you want?" "We have a search warrant." and he hands one of the printed papers to me. I take it, I read it and I find it to be a printed form, containing indeed a search warrant, with my name on it handwritten in ink.

"Search at four o'clock in the morning? It's a weird time for this. Can't you come back later, at seven o'clock?" "Impossible. We have to carry out the order immediately."

I open the door and invite him into my study; I see, at the same time, that another four representatives of the secret police are waiting in the yard. Before entering, he turns around in the doorway and makes a sign to the others; three of them come up the stairs and enter, behind him, in the hall. I invite him to take a seat and ask him in which order, with which room, he wants to start the search. He answers: " With this very room, your study", but he adds immediately, "You have to go with us to the Ministry of the Interior" and he hands me a second printed paper. I reply: "You cannot search in my absence; how can I know that one of your people won't slip a manifesto or a gun among my things?" "The members of your family will be present during the search; as for you, we kindly ask you to dress and come with us."

Meanwhile, my wife enters the room; I explain to her what the situation is and the officer assures her that the search will be done only in her presence. The other three agents are in the office now. I know one of them: He is an agent of the in the 31st District, in Știrbey-Vodă Street, short and wall-eyed. He fixes me with the good eye, while the other eye floats away. The second agent is tall, with a handsome face, and blue angelic eyes. He wears a leather coat to his knees as some of the fascists used to wear. The third one is also tall, well built; I found out later, in July 1955, that he was a professional boxer. The fourth agent remained in the yard and he supervised the back entrance and the basement windows. The officer goes to the telephone, dials a number and, after a few seconds, says to the other end: "Alright." I couldn't tell what number he dialed; I suppose it was one of the offices at the Ministry of the Interior, where he had to communicate immediately about whether the subject was found at his home.

I go upstairs, to the bathroom, accompanied by the agent wearing the leather coat. While I shave myself and take a shower he doesn't take his eyes off of me; he keeps his right hand permanently in his pocket, probably holding a gun. Maybe he is afraid that I will attack him, hit him in the head; on the other hand he probably wants to prevent any suicide attempts. There were such cases. In 1940, in the fascist period, in Iași, Petre Andrei, former minister of education, swallowed poison while he dressed, and died within seconds, in front of the agent who came to arrest him and take him to Bucharest. Maybe Colonel Nicu Boianu, son-in-law of Nicușor Săveanu, took poison when the secret police came to take him; the fact is that he fell dead, in front of the house, before getting into the car. Some people say that he died of heart disease, which is possible, because he was ill before.

I tried to find out from the agent who doesn't take his eyes off of me, why I have to go to the Ministry of the Interior; he answers shortly that he doesn't know. When I come out of the bathroom, I find in the next room, sitting on chairs, my wife's parents, Maria and Simion Mehedinți, who live with us, and my brother-in-law Emil Mehedinți who had happened to stay over that night.

The officer asks them one after the other: "Who are you?". Each of them tells him who they are; my father-in-law stares at the officer as if imprinting the face in his mind. "You are free" concludes the officer, after he settles the matter of their identity; "you can go to your rooms". I embrace them and go downstairs; I find my wife there, arranging some of my clothes in a suitcase; she had asked the officer whether I would need such things and he had given an affirmative answer; I understand that my visit to the Ministry of the Interior will last a while. My daughter prepares black coffee; I offer the officer a cup, and he refuses politely.

I remember my hunting rifle and the hundreds of bullets I have in the house; in order to avoid any question and suspicion towards my family, I show the officer the permit to carry a gun, stamped for the current year, and the hunting permit, delivered by the society I'm a member of – the Society of Sector of Yellow, headquartered at the state bank. The officer immediately notes the number of the gun permit in a notebook.

I say good-bye to my wife and my daughter; my eldest son is not in town. He works as a foreman on a building site in Andrășești (Ialomița County); he must come to Bucharest this afternoon. My youngest son is abroad, in Paris studying architecture. At the moment of separation, my wife whispers, in French so that the agent cannot understand: "Tu rentreras" (You will come back home). I will remember these magic words very often during my long detention years in the cell of Sighet penitentiary; these words will help me to live and hope even when everything seemed hopeless. I take my suitcase and my coat and, accompanied by the officer, I leave the house. I descend the stairs and cross the yard. My wife looks at me out of the bedroom windows; I turn around and see her once again before going out the gate; I don't anticipate at that time that more than five years will pass before I see her again.

We walk down Berzei Street to the left; the officer walks near me, keeping one of his hands in his pocket. We turn on Virgiliu Street and, just after the corner, we run into a police car that was waiting for us. The driver sleeps; you can see that he had had many drives to make during the night. My companion awakens him and, without a word, he makes a sign. I stay in the back seat on the left; we drive on Știrbei Vodă Street, cross Luterană Street and drive up to Calea Victoriei. The city is still asleep; I don't see more than three or four people on our way. It is a splendid May morning, the sky is clear and bright; a warm wind blows gently; the trees are completely green. I look at the houses and gardens we pass by and, again, I don't anticipate I won't see them for a long time. We arrive on Calea Victoriei; we turn right and once we are at Piața Palatului, we see the massive building of the Ministry of the Interior. We pass near the main entrance which, painted in black and having ornamental plants, looks like a vault entrance to me. We turn twice to the left and we are in the Ministry's yard, in front of a service entrance.

I get out of the car; the officer turns me over to a tall agent, then he gets into the car again and probably returns to my home in order to be present for the search.

At the Ministry of the Interior

The tall man to whom I was turned over asks me to give him my eyeglasses and instead gives me a pair of blind glasses, having black metallic discs as lenses. I can't see anything; guided by the agents' hand, I descend stairs, I take many steps, I descend more steps, then again and take a few steps and enter, finally, a room. The glasses are taken off and I am given my own glasses. In front of me I see an under-officer, wearing a uniform, sitting at a desk; he doesn't wear boots but instead wears some house shoes made of felt or cloth so that he moves without making a sound. The room has no windows; also the light bulb is on all the time.

First of all, the under-officer settles the matter of my identity and fills out a form: Last name and first name, domicile, parents names; my profession, my wife's and my children's names.

After this he takes my tie and shoelaces, preventative measures against a suicide attempt. Then he inspects my suitcase: he takes out my razor and an unopened packet of Gillette blades and puts them away; he also takes out a bottle of cologne and two French magazines that I have taken from home believing that I would be able to read; finally he asks for my eyeglasses and my wedding ring. Initially I oppose this: the eyeglasses are prescribed by a doctor, which is a reality; without them I cannot distinguish someone face from twelve feet away; "It doesn't matter" the under-officer answers, "You won't need them." As for the wedding ring I pretend not to be able to remove it; the man doesn't give up and, with some effort, he removes it. This is the thing that hurts most; I have the impression of being torn away from my family, my wife and my children. I protest vehemently against this confiscation; the under-officer assures me that the wedding ring will be returned to me at the end. Later I will understand the reason for this measure: it was taken in order to prevent a warden from being bribed with this golden object. For the same reason my silver cufflinks, my watch and three thousand lei are taken away from me. I sign a receipt specifying the belongings taken away and then, wearing the same dark glasses and accompanied by the same tall man, I am led to an elevator. I expect that we will go down; I had heard, many times, in previous years, about the famous underground cells, about the underground "floors" of the Ministry of the Interior. Alexandrini, former Minister of Finance, had told me that he spent several days in such a cell, when he was arrested – for a short time – in 1949. To my surprise, the elevator is going up instead of down. After a few seconds we stop; I think we are at the third floor. I take a few steps and I enter another room. The dark glasses are removed and I see that I am in a room that has a window masked by a heavy curtain. I am given a chair; in front of me, on another chair, at a desk, sits an agent wearing a blue uniform. This is a bear-like man, with a red, almost purple face and with frightening hands; these are the hands of a professional strangler. I cannot take my eyes off of them: he keeps them stretched out on the desk, in sight, as if to make me understand that it is dangerous to anger him. In fact, I realize that any attempt at opposition or escape is senseless. Even if, having one chance out of a billion, I succeeded in escaping from this room it wouldn't help at all. These men have infallible methods: they immediately arrest your wife and children, so that you come by yourself to surrender in order to make them release your family.

I stay in this room for about two and a half hours; the agent who watches me doesn't say a word. Judging from the noise coming from outside I think our room is facing the street: Is this Academiei Street or Calea Victoriei? Because of the heavy curtain I cannot see anything outside.

Because, on the one hand, I was not taken to an underground cell, and on the other hand in this room *there is no bed*, I think I won't remain here.

On the wall behind me there is a map of the railroads; I examine this map and my eyes linger – I don't know why – on the northern part of Transylvania. Will I be sent there? Or, as I had been told about others arrested, will I be transported to the Soviet Union?

This is a tormenting question that I cannot answer. But, in fact, why am I arrested? What am I charged with?

I try to find out something from the agent who watches me, but I don't get a response. He looks at me with bovine, expressionless eyes; he gives the impression that he doesn't even understand Romanian. However, when after two hours, I tell him I need to go to the toilet, the man stands up and makes a sign to follow him. This time, I am not given the glasses; we go into a hall, take fifteen steps to the left and stop in front of a door that the agent opens, gesturing to me to go in. He remains in front of the half-opened door and, after a minute, he leads me back into the room we came from.

It must be seven or quarter past seven; how long will this waiting last? While I'm thinking of the details of the mornings events the door opens suddenly and an agent – he seems to be an under-officer – makes a sign to follow him. I take my suitcase and coat and walk down the hall to the elevator I came by. I find here Al. Popescu-Necșești Popescu-Necșești and Napoleon Crețu, old acquaintances; the latter was with me in college, he in Romanian language and I in History and Geography. We greet each other briefly; immediately after that appear successively Radu Portocală, Manolescu-Strunga, Pantelimon Halippa and Tancred Constantinescu. There are seven of us and with the agent, eight. The elevator goes down and stops at the ground floor. A few steps and I am again near the service entrance.

In the yard, in front of this entrance, there is a van parked so that its' back doors are by the entrance. A second van waits parallel to the first, six feet away. We are assigned numbers – I am number seven – and are told that we will be addressed by these numbers.

When I hear my number I step forward; two agents, one at my right and another at my left, accompany me to the vans' door and motion for me to get inside.

I enter a central corridor; on the left I see five individual boxes which seem to be occupied because their doors' are closed; on the right, in the middle of the corridor, there is a door to a long and narrow room, the equivalent of the boxes on the other side. In this room there is a wooden bench on which we sit one after weeks ago; he had just returned from the hospital when he was arrested. General Samsonovici is agitated and he says he is suffocating; he wants the communication door with the central corridor – a half open sliding door – to be completely open. Hearing him, one of the agents appears in the entrance and with a sharp tone, he threatens that if the General doesn't stop talking immediately he will close the door completely. He even makes a demonstration: he closes it completely; we find ourselves in total darkness; we cannot see each other anymore. After thirty seconds, the door is half opened again; this time General Samsonovici stays quiet, he doesn't have any requirements anymore.

A bucket is brought in for "making number 1", as people in Transylvania used to say; then comes a basket with food; everyone is given a packet with two loaves of bread, two helpings of white cheese (30-40 grams each!) and two helpings of marmalade (the same weight!). This means that our journey will last longer, that it won't end in one day. But, in this case, where are we going? The fellows in the van make all kinds of assumptions: some of them think they're taking us to the Soviet Union – Crețu is among them – by boat on the Danube from Oltenița or Giurgiu; others think we'll go to Aiud, others to Bucovina, others to Northern Transylvania. Portocală believes that they cannot take us out of the country: it would cause a scandal with the United Nations and the Russians are not interested in provoking such a thing. We will be able to have a better idea about this when we get out of Bucharest.

For the moment we are waiting for the other van to be loaded. I keep thinking of what is going on at home with the search. I heard about it much later, in July of 1955; my wife told me that immediately after we left for the Ministry of the Interior, two of the agents started to inspect the library in my study, taking down each book. They couldn't find anything. They continued with the upstairs library and my sons' library: with the same negative result. When they went to the library in the basement they had no more patience; it was already two in the afternoon and they didn't bother to inspect it. The officer who took me to the Ministry returned to my house at about ten o'clock – he probably had other similar operations to carry out meanwhile. He came with another man who started, very nervously, to inspect the paintings, to turn them over, and knock on their frames. Eventually he concentrated his attention on the armchair where my wife sat. The other agents were looking with curiosity and almost with compassion at the new man; though at a certain moment, when he had his back turned, they grimaced at his procedures. At about 2:30 in the afternoon, the secret police team left the house, taking with them only a few of my belongings, among them my brochure about Transylvania, printed in 1942-43 by the Ministry of Propaganda in six languages.

The other van is loaded now; of course we don't know who is in it but there must be former ministers. The composition of the group in our van shows clearly the character of the measures taken. It does not concern certain persons for personal guilt, but *an entire category*: the former high dignitaries – ministers, state secretaries, deputy state secretaries, belonging to all the political parties and former party heads – with the exception, of course, of those who joined the communist party or its' offshoots such as the Ploughmens' Front and the National Popular Party. At fifteen minutes to eight, our van starts, followed by the other at a distance of about sixty feet or so.

The journey to Sighet

We drive out of the yard of the Ministry of the Interior, enter Wilson Street and turn to the left on Brătianu Boulevard and head to Kiseleff Avenue. Thus, the hypothesis about Olteniţa or Giurgiu followed by the journey on the Danube was wrong. When we pass by Atena Street, the public clock there shows 7:48. The city's life is fully ongoing. Numerous pedestrians, crowded tramway stops, street vendors, children, youths, I see everything within several seconds through the two half opened doors: the door that opens on the central corridor and the entrance door at the back of the van. I have, from this point of view, the best position. The fellows in boxes and those who sit in the middle and on the opposite side of the bench cannot see anything of what happens outside. Maybe it's better for them, because the contrast between the free life bustling on the other side of the vans' walls and my miserable position, crushed in the narrow space of the bench and tormented by the gloomy prospects ahead, gives me a very depressed mood.

We arrive in Piaţa Victoriei; I catch, for a moment, the sight of the end of Buzeşti Street on which I walked so many times on my way home to Berzei Street; who knows when and if I will ever walk home that way again. Who knows when I will see the lime trees in flower again at Jianu, the national park and the necklace of lakes around it! We enter Kiseleff Avenue; leaving behind the Arch of Triumph, the hippodrome, and Mioriţa fountain and turn on to the road to Ploeşti. From time to time I see the other van and two cars that follow.

We are now by Tîncăbeşti; we go down a slope: I see for a short time the lake where I spent so many pleasant hours fishing. Very close to the road, at the edge of a thicket, in a small primitive boat there is a fisherman with two fishing poles. I wonder whether he observes the passing van, whether he realizes what this dreary vehicle means with its' fake windows painted on its' outside. Probably not; his attention must be concentrated now completely on his fishing poles. Last year, in August, while I was in a boat fishing on the Tîncăbeşti lake I saw, passing on the same road, four similar vans. These weird vehicles puzzled me at the time: but I must confess that I didn't imagine how much suffering and horror such a convoy means. We come nearer to Ploești; which way will we go after we cross the town? To Brașov or to Buzău? This is the issue that we discuss on the bench. Those who are in the boxes cannot take part in our conversation because their doors are almost permanently closed; an extra penalty!

We cross the bridge over the railroad, drive onto the beautiful boulevard that links the Southern station with the center of the town and then turn left. So it is clear now: we are heading to Brașov. We are less worried now because the other direction, to Moldova, also implies the possibility of crossing Prut river to the Soviet Union. I'm not thinking – in this moment – that this thing is still possible and that from the Sighet penitentiary to the border with the Soviet Union – Tisa river – the distance is not bigger than one kilometer. But nobody imagines yet, at this time, that we will go to the extreme north of the country.

We leave behind Cîmpina, Breaza, Comarnic, Posada; we are near Sinaia. The van stops on the right side of the road by a fountain with marvelous water; we are allowed to get out for a few minutes; the accompanying agents and officers stand around us. There are three agents in our van; two of them are surely Jews if the physiognomy and the accent can be used as criteria. In the cars there are officers and there seems to be a doctor.

Laying on the green grass near the fountain I see in the valley, a personal train going to Ploești. I reckon again as I did at the Ministry of the Interior: What if I tried to escape? I would cross the road and slide down the slope to the railway. The attempt – I realize immediately – has no chance to be successful; before getting to the slope I would be shot by one of the agents. And even if I could manage to get into the valley safe and alive, and disappear in the thick forest covering the mountain, I still couldn't resolve anything. The secret police would immediately arrest my family – wife and children – and I would be forced to surrender in order to avoid bigger torment for them: I heard many times that family members were beaten and even tortured in order to give away where the husband or son is hidden.

We start again. I catch, for a moment, the sight of Sinaia Casino; I cannot see anything of Bușteni, Azuga and Predeal because the agents closed the entrance door to the van, I don't know the reason why. We go down into the Timiș valley, cross Brașov through a suburb, not through the center, and then head to Făgăraș. Between these two towns, we enter a secondary road and stop for a half an hour for lunch.

We get out of the van and sit on the grass, on the edge of a ditch. But nobody can eat. I feel like I have a lump in my throat preventing me from swallowing. I realize it's something psychological; I look at the others: nobody touches the food; the packets are put back intact.

On the other hand the agents eat with appetite: they open a can of meat; they also have other food and white bread.

I talk with Crețu about our destination. He thinks it might be a camp; but also, he says, that he doesn't preclude the possibility of some villas in a mountain resort being arranged for us. "In fact, a few months holiday in a mountain area would be very convenient for me" he concludes. Crețu was imprisoned before, from September 1944 to January 1945, i.e. for five months, in a camp in Caracal. He suffered a lot because of the insects, especially the bedbugs. He tells me how he was arrested last night. He left with only his briefcase and a sweater his daughter gave him.

We stop in Făgărași in order to get gas. The van goes pretty fast but it also makes many stops; and whenever it starts again it does so with repeated jolts. Alimănișteanu especially suffers because of these jolts; his repeated request to be allowed to stay facing the direction of movement is brutally denied. At one of the stops I notice that the officers opened an envelope; it probably contained instructions concerning the route to be followed.

I have been told that, in such situations, not only the prisoners but even the drivers and the officers don't know the destination of the convoy; the route is successively indicated by envelopes which are handed to the officers at certain stopping points. This practice was probably adopted in order to make any attack attempt impossible. This proves once again that the regime doesn't trust its' own people, not even policemen who were selected for being committed.

Mistrust, mutual spying and informing are in fact characteristic of the current regime.

After Sibiu, that we cross without stopping, we head north. After we pass Alba-Iulia, we begin to talk again about our destination. Some of us believe that it is Aiud, with its' famous prison; others affirm that, nevertheless, we will cross the border to the Soviet Union. This makes Pantelimon Halippa make the following epigram: "Green leaves of a sour berry tree/they're taking us to Aiud/but I'm afraid that, as I suppose/they will make us cross Tisa".[24]

The most talkative of all of us is Manolescu-Strunga Manolescu-Strunga; he tells us all kinds of stories, without omitting – given his well known temperament – their erotic side. He only has one apprehension: in his library there are many forbidden books, Hitler's *Mein Kampf* is among them. He also has a regret: this morning a friend was supposed to visit him and bring him some money for some things he had sold, and take other things to sell in the "flea market". This "noble institution" – characteristic to the communist regime – prospers every Sunday in the Colentina district; you can see there men and women belonging to the upper and middle bourgeoisie selling the most valuable things in their houses; buyers are peasants and functionaries of the new regime, "the new aristocracy".

Radu Portocală sits hunched over in his place and he presses his stomach with his hand; the jolts caused by the drive do not help his wound which is newly healed. But he doesn't complain. He bears the pain with stoicism. On the other hand, General Samsonovici is permanently nervous; he says he cannot stay on the bench; he sits down on the floor, requires the door opening into the corridor to be completely open, he keeps calling one of the agents, wants to get out of the car, in conclusion he has the behavior which doesn't suit an old soldier but rather a spoiled child. The result is that, eventually, the warden snaps at him in a tough way and Manolescu-Strunga Manolescu-Strunga warns him that his attitude might lead to the complete closing of both doors, and this would make the journey even more painful. Following this double intervention he calms down for a while. Halippa tells us with melancholy and humor how he was imprisoned, a long time ago, by the Russians; he hadn't believed a time would come for him to be imprisoned by his own countrymen in Transylvania.

It is getting dark; at about eight o'clock, we stop in a lonely place, again on a secondary road, for dinner. This time, I manage to swallow a few bites of bread; the cheese is so salted and dried that it really cannot be eaten; the marmalade is finished.

At about ten to half past ten in the evening, we arrive on the

---

[24] In the original Romanian version: "Foaie verde de agud/Ne duc măre la Aiud;/Dar mă tem că, pasă-mi-sa (sic)/O să ne treacă și Tisa."

outskirts of a town where we find an institution intensely lit by powerful electric bulbs. We see something that looks like a barbed wire net. Is it Aiud? None of us can say precisely, and the agent refuses to give us any explanation. We stop in the neighborhood of this place, on a secondary road again, and we remain here for the night. Because of the narrow space and the suffocating heat we cannot sleep; we stay and bear this torture until five o'clock in the morning when the van starts again. If the place where we spent the night was Aiud, it's good that we didn't remain in that frightening prison; we didn't know that there was a place even worse reserved for us, from the point of view of psychological as well as material treatment.

We keep driving all the morning, without us being able to guess our route. The general direction is northerly; we are not able to read the signs at the entrances of the towns. Only at about one o'clock, Crețu sees for a moment, at the intersection of the road and the railroad tracks, a sign saying: "To Carei". So we are in northern Crișana. The scenery becomes plain; the road is no longer cement; the jolts are more numerous.

At about half past one, the van stops again on a secondary road, for lunch. We get out and see, to the northeast, on the horizon, a chain of dark mountains, covered with forests. I reckon they must be the mountains that separate northern Transylvania from Maramureș. We all look with apprehension at these gloomy heights. What if we, however, cross Tisa and plunge into the Soviet chaos? I remember what my wife told me on the morning of November 23, 1945, when the ship bringing us from Istanbul was preparing to enter the Constanța sea port. She was looking at the porters lined up on the quay, wearing on their chest a large red Soviet star, and she told me in a voice that I will never forget: "Do you see how the thread pulls us to Siberia?"

What if her prophecy comes true, if her instinct was right? But anyway, what can I do now? Let it be as God wills it!

Crețu takes me aside and, emotionally, he whispers: "Don't laugh at me, but if we cross the border, I would like to kiss this country's' soil before leaving it". I answer: "How can you imagine I can laugh at such a gesture?"

I still continue to believe, together with Portocală, that they won't take us to the Soviet Union.

We sit on the grass to eat. One of the agents opens two cans of meat and hands them to us. But we have no knife, no fork, no spoon. I look around me and see, a few feet away, near the road, a wild plum tree; I tear off a branch with two points, I strip the branch and improvise a fork; with this we can take the pieces of meat out of the can. I exchange a few words with Dumitru Alimănişteanu Alimănişteanu and general Racoviţă-Jandarmul. The latter is eighty-four years old; but he holds up well; with the help of the improvised fork, he pays homage to the canned meat.

While we eat, we see four vans similar to ours passing on the main road. This makes me realize that these arrest are more widespread than I'd thought; the number of those arrested in Bucharest – figuring that each vans "load" is as large as ours -must be between seventy and eighty. In fact, this number will be bigger because people arrested in the following days will arrive in Sighet later, at the beginning of July.

A few minutes later, a truck shows up, loaded with a group of young workers who stand and sing. The truck is decorated with a red banner and a tri-color one. When the workers see the van and our group on the grass, the song becomes lower and lower and then they stop. They stare at us and look impressed.

The van starts and after about two hours we begin to drive uphill. So we arrive at the mountains that we saw at noon when we stopped for lunch. The road goes through a beautiful forest; now and then we cross brooks. The suffocating heat in the van – some of us wear only our shirts – seems to abate. The physical weariness and the nervous tension grow bigger and bigger. If only we would arrive at our destination sooner!

Portocală doesn't feel well; I call one of the agents who, to encourage him, says: "There's a big hospital where we're going and you will be taken care of".

But when I ask him where we are and what is the end of our journey he answers the first question with a lie: "We are in Moldova". To the second question he answers: "We arrive soon, before dark". Indeed, at about half past six we enter a town; we don't see any sign; after a few minutes, the van stops in front of a high wall and a locked black metal gate. We wait here for a half an hour, in an infernal heat. Both vans doors were closed by the agents, therefore, because of the hot metal walls and the lack of air circulation the temperature continues to rise; it must be 104 degrees; it becomes hard to even breath.

Finally, the gate opens; the van enters. We make a new, shorter stop in the yard and then get out one by one. I realize immediately that we are in a large prison, with a ground floor and two upper floors.

THE SIGHET PENITENTIARY

The arrival and imprisonment in Sighet

The building is massive; the rows of barred windows give it a grim aspect. We are led one by one into a long and high room, it is the height of the entire building, which looks like the nave of a gothic church. On the right and on the left there are doors covered with iron and having heavy bolts; exactly above them, on the second and third floors there are identical doors. A wooden catwalk gives access to the doors on each floor; at about twelve feet – the height of the first floor – a net made of thick wire covers the entire room: this is in order to prevent prisoners from committing suicide by leaping from the second or third floor. When you see all this a chill runs up your spine.

There is a group of three officers waiting at the entrance of this room. One of them, tall and well fed, who seems to have the highest rank of the three – Captain or Major – holds a paper in his hand; probably, our names and our cell assignments are written on it.

When my turn comes, the tall officer asks me what my name is. I tell him; he looks on the list and makes a check with a pencil, then he asks again: "Are you the author of the History of Romanians?" After I answer yes, he considers it appropriate to make a remark that he thinks is witty and conforms with the "party line": "Nowadays the history of Romania is written differently". "It's possible" I respond, "but our history remains only one history." He sends an enlisted man to accompany me to the second floor; I only ascend a few steps on the rocky staircase leading to the second floor, when the tall officer calls me back and tells the man to take me to cell number 21 on the first floor. The cell is situated on the right side looking from the entrance towards the back of the floor. It is the fifth cell from the entrance.

During the same Sunday afternoon (May 7, 1950) the other vans arrive from Bucharest. In one of them were eighteen people, among them I mention Nicolae Sibiceanu, Victor Papacostea, General Niculae Marinescu, General Cihoski, C.C. Zamfirescu, and Florian Ştefănescu-Goangă. Later, in 1952, I learned details from the first two of these men about their journey to the prison. The details are as follows: Their van was not divided into three parts like ours, it had no boxes. There was only one room with a circular bench. During the journey, General Cihoski had a nervous breakdown and started to talk continually. He imagined himself as a young officer solving different job problems; he saw himself commanding the soldiers or giving directions and penalties to his subordinates; and finally, he saw himself "flirting" and making declarations of love. The film of his entire life unfolded in front of his companions. It was an embarrassing spectacle, and at times really tragic; once an elite officer, now with his mind wandering, he was speaking endlessly. He died, a short time after he arrived at Sighet, without ever recovering.

This van didn't stop at all during the night, and its' route wasn't the same as ours. The agents who came with the van behaved with brutality; during the night they simulated loading their guns, wanting to suggest that the moment of execution was near.

With another van arrived Constantin Argetoianu, the brothers Alexandru and Ion Lapedatu, August Filip and others. A third van brought Gheorghe Strat, the Generals Glatz and Achille Diculescu, Dr. Ciugureanu, D. Caracostea, Budurescu and others; eighteen people all together. During the journey, near Turdea, Dr. Ciugureanu from Basarabia had cerebral congestion; he was taken out of the van and transported to the hospital in Turdea where he died soon after. He was the first of the many victims following the arrests of the night of May 5-6, 1950. From Gherla came, on the evening of May 6th, Romulus Pop, who had led the refugee commission during the Sănătescu and Rădescu governments. He made the journey handcuffed and wearing dark eyeglasses.

From Timişoara came Dumitru Nistor, deputy state secretary in the Ministry of the Interior during the same governments, along with Coriolan Băran, Titus Popovici and Sever Bocu. Later, in about two months, a new group came from Bucharest. This group included Nicolae Cornăţeanu, Victor Slăvescu, Victor Moldovan, Zenovie Pâclişanu, general Racoviţă (who was the Minister of War after August 23, 1944), Dinu Simian, Admiral Georgescu, General Popovici (Epure!), Mihail Romaşcanu (former high commissioner at the Dept. of prices), D. V. Toni and Asra Bercovici (ex-director of the *Liberalul* newspaper of the liberal party). They were arrested within about a month and a half of May 6, 1950.

Thus, Nicolae Cornăţeanu for example, who worked in Scorţaru in Brăila County, was arrested there on the afternoon of Monday, May 8; Victor Slăvescu stayed free for a month after our arrest; the same for general Racoviță. Dinu Simian managed to stay free for more than a month after our arrest because on his identity card was written, by mistake, the name Constantin Simion, although the birthplace was registered Săliște, which was correct. Indeed, who would believe that Dinu Simian living in Rîmnicu Vîlcea is the same person as Constantin Simion from Săliște. Add to this the fact that he had changed his address; he was arrested at a friends' whom he went to visit. This latter group stayed at the Ministry of the Interior in very hard conditions, crowded at the beginning in a cell for one person, sleeping like sardines, not having the possibility to go to the toilet except for at certain times, and not having enough air. This first stage at the Ministry of the Interior was for them like a month in hell.

From the corridor they heard at times during the night, the cries of those who were "interrogated"; they even heard lamenting women's voices.

Also arriving after us was the group of around Uniate priests. I know the names of some of them: Rusu, Sîrbu, Sălăjan, Vultur (who was also a professor in Blaj), and four bishops, namely: Hossu, Suciu, Rusu and Frențiu; to these was added the catholic bishop of Timișoara, Augustin Pacha.

First days, first impressions

The cell in which I was imprisoned, on the evening of May 7, 1950, was a small one for one or at maximum two persons. It was fifteen feet long, six feet wide and eleven feet high. The lower edge of the window, situated six feet above the floor, did not permit you to see the soil in the yard. So you couldn't see people outside, only the surrounding wall, the watch tower, and a part of the building and the sky. The ceiling of the cell was arched – when the building was constructed, in 1896, reinforced concrete was not yet in use – the floor was made of fir. Under the window, there were three pipes parallel to the floor and running through the walls that separate the cell from the neigh-boring cells; these pipes served as radiators. The door, opposite the window, was covered with an iron sheet; at eye level the door had a small circular opening, equipped with an outer shutter; through this opening the prison staff could supervise the prisoner in the cell without being seen by him. Under the observation opening there was a rectangular opening; a shutter that opened out and downwards. Through this opening – some call it "vasistas" – a warden can give the food to the prisoner without opening the door. The bed is on one end of the cell directly under the window and is parallel to the door. It is made of iron and has a straw mattress, sheet, a blanket and a pillow filled with straw in a pillowcase. The sight of the bed, the chance to sleep like a human being after a sleepless night and two tiresome days of travel, relieved the nervous tension I was feeling. I lay on the bed immediately and had almost fallen asleep when the door of the cell opened suddenly and two people entered. One of them, in civilian clothes, wearing a shirt with a "bubikragen" collar, looks at me insistently but without saying a word; the other one, in a blue uniform – a wardens uniform – holds a big pitcher of water in his hand; the sides of the pitcher are damp. "Drink" the warden says and hands me the pitcher. I drink directly from it – it is neither a glass nor a cup – the water is excellent and very cold. I lay again on the bed and I'm ready to go to sleep when the door opens again – the door always opens violently, with noise – and the civilian from before asks: "Do you want any food?" I thank him and say that I don't need any; in fact, I didn't want anything but to rest. I take off my clothes, I put my pajamas on and lay on the bed, under the blanket; this time, nothing else happens. I am seized by a leaden sleep; when I awake, it is morning outside; I see the blue sky in the background and the bars of the window in the foreground and I suddenly remember where I am. I feel a twinge in my right shoulder blade; I look at the window and see that the lower right pane is missing. During the night, because I was sweating, the wind had gotten to me and that's why I have this pain.

It must be at least six o'clock in the morning; one cannot feel any movement in the corridor or in the yard. I look around me and cannot see any arrangement or receptacle which would permit the satisfaction of inexorable needs. What can I do? I wait a few minutes and then I bang the door with my fist; I also hear around me, in other cells, similar banging. After a while, the door opens violently – as usual – and another warden, not the same one as last night, snaps at me: "What do you want?" it is obvious that he considers such a banging "against the rules" and he is angry; but there wasn't any other way I could have behaved. I tell him what I want; he glares at me and answers shortly: "Wait". This is a word that I would hear very often from now on; I could say that this is the word that best summarized our life in prison. After fifteen minutes, the door opens again and the same nasty warden – whom my suffering fellows will later call B-1, i.e. "Beast number 1" – tells me: "Come with me to the toilet!" I follow him down the hall, to the entrance; on the left, on the same side as my cell, is the "toilet": a hole cut in the dirty cement of the floor. Water was nonexistent. The warden stands in the door and watches me; not even thirty seconds went by and he tells me in the same sharp tone: "Come on, hurry up!" I return to my cell and I ask myself what are the older people doing, especially those who suffer from prostate problems.

After another fifteen minutes – it must be seven or half past seven – the door opens again. In the doorway I see the civilian from last night and two wardens who carry a wicker basket with small pieces of bread and a dish with bits of bacon fat in it. The civilian hands me a piece of bread – it may weigh 35-40 grams, and a piece of bacon fat – 10 or 12 grams. I take them and, in less than two minutes, I finish them. Is this the "breakfast"? It's not bad, for the prison; but I have the impression that this is something exceptional, that it replaces the usual food for the first morning. Of course, the administration didn't have the time yet to make the necessary arrangements for the rather large number of "boarders" that arrived last night; we don't yet have a tin cup, for water, a plate or even a mess kit. These things will be given out during the morning: a 375 milliliter enameled tin cup and a enameled mess tin able to hold one and a half liters, for food. The enamel is chipped on both; the tin is greasy; the one who ate from it last night didn't make the effort to remove the grease on the bottom and on the edges. Not having water at hand, I take a handkerchief out of my suitcase and begin to clean the two dishes. Well, let's say I cleaned them as best I could, although any housekeeper would be indignant at the result; but what can you do without water? As for the handkerchief, dirty with grease, I put it for the moment on the edge of the window; I will wash it when I have the wherewithal to do so.

The door opens again: they distribute bread. I receive a, theoretically, 250 gram loaf, with the explanation that this is my helping for twenty-four hours; so it has to be enough for today's lunch, dinner and for tomorrow morning. In reality, the loaf is not much bigger than 220-230 grams (ca. 8 oz).

I wonder where I am, in which locality. I hear the church bells; there are three different bells; thus it would seem to be a rather important town; the size of the prison is also a sign of this. Judging from the way we traveled, the fact that we, at the end of the journey, crossed some mountains, it would seem that we are in the north of Transylvania, in Maramureș. But what if the mountains were the Apuseni mountains, and if we turned to the west without noticing, as someone affirmed yesterday in the van? An argument against this is the sign "To Carei" that Crețu saw yesterday, at about one o'clock, before we drove up into the mountains that were *in the north*. Thus, it is highly probable that we are in Maramureș, namely in the capitol of this county, *Sighet*. The question of where we are was considered by all those who were brought here; all kinds of answers were given. I learn -later – from Cornățeanu (or from Romașcanu?) that some people believed that we were in Caransebeș, in Banat; others tended to believe we were in Bucovina. Silviu Dragomir told me that he recognized the tower of a church and he said from the beginning that the town where we stopped was Sighet.

Meanwhile, it has become noon. I hear a bell ringing in the inside of the prison and soon after that the cell door opens, with the usual noise. I see a warden – different from the one that morning – who calls me with a calm voice: "Come here and get food". He takes beans with a ladle out of a tub, its opening is larger than its' base, and puts them in my mess tin. "Do you want more?" "No", I respond, "Thank you", and I withdraw to my bed. The door closes; the bolt – only one, outside – is drawn. I have neither knife nor fork. These are dangerous objects that could be used for suicide and, therefore, they are forbidden in prison. I eat with a spoon; later I will use this also for cutting meat. The beans are cooked with pork grease; they don't taste bad; however, I only eat half of the beans and leave the rest. This first lunch, alone, with a tin on my knees, is very depressing; I think of the thousands of meals I've had with my family, around a table arranged with all the necessary things for a civilized life. At the time I thought that everything was absolutely normal – how could it be otherwise? – and I didn't appreciate, or I didn't appreciate enough, this aspect of my happy family life. This is the way man is doomed to be: to not appreciate what he has and, always dissatisfied, want something better.

The door opens again: "Go to the toilet and go take your water supply" the warden who served the food tells me. I go into the hall, now I know the way; when I return, I find at about six feet from my cell, near the door of the neighboring cell – number 20 – a tub – a bit larger than the food tub – from which I take a cup of water. If I had my tin emptied, if I had eaten all the beans, I could take water in it; now I must be content with only the water in the cup. Back in the cell, I drink half of the water and save the rest. What am I to do now? There's no place where I can empty the left-over beans; I cannot wash, even halfway, the handkerchief, because I risk using up the water. So the only thing I can do is wait and see how things will develop.

I lay on the bed again; my thoughts run to my family at home. What are they doing now? Will there follow, now that I am arrested, all kinds of difficulties and misery for them? Will the children be able to continue their studies? These are tormenting questions that I cannot answer anyway. I begin to pace in the cell: from the door to the window and back, from the window to the door; six steps in one direction and seven in the other. I pace like a robot, I keep pacing for hours in order to get tired and chase away my bad thoughts. And as soon as I sit on the bed, the same tormenting questions begin drilling into my mind.

It must be half past five to a quarter to six. The prisons' bell rings again: it's time for dinner, the same warden calls it "ojina". As food, there are beans again, this time "less thick" than at lunch. The warden pours a ladle full of beans over the left-over ones. "Why didn't you finish your beans[25] ?" he asks me, without meanness, even with a sort of sympathy. "Because I cannot!" I answer. "That's not good, eat it, it's good food; later you will be so hungry that you will chew on the walls". I thought it was just a figure of speech; but he was right; many times, during the following months, I thought of what he had said. I learned, by chance, a few days later, the name of this warden: he was named Pintea. I heard other wardens on duty calling him by this name.

I don't finish my helping again this time. I had just finished eating when the door opened; I hear the same order as at noon: "Go to the toilet and go take your water supply". This time, I take the tin with me; I empty it in the toilet, I rinse it with the water I kept from lunch and then I can take water in both dishes. This is progress: I will be able to wash my handkerchief. After I wash it, I put it in the window to replace the missing pane of glass; then I move the bed away from the window so the wind won't get to me during the night.

At seven in the evening the wardens' shift: the day warden leaves and the night one comes on duty; everyone is on duty for twelve hours. After he takes over, the night warden locks the cell *with the key* and closes the bolt; during the day, usually, only the bolt is shut. At nine o'clock in the evening it is "lights out": it is a figure of speech because for the moment, there are no lights; the electrical system in the cells doesn't work therefore in the night we sleep *without light.* This lack is a big advantage for the prisoners; we will realize that later when, after the electrical system is repaired, a powerful bulb is on all night long.

I slept uninterruptedly until five in the morning when I am awakened by the prison bell: thus, this bell marks the essential moments in our twenty-four hour day: the reveille, breakfast, lunch, dinner and lights out. When, later, the "roll call" is established, the bell will also announce the two daily times: at seven a.m. and p.m.

During the second night, I have an impressive dream: I am with my wife, in Braşov, in a big pastry shop. There is a large, elegant room with crystal topped tables and couches covered with red plush

---

[25] mashed beans

upholstery; we order cakes; extraordinary music over-flows with waves of harmony; it is one of the pleasant times in life when you enjoy, without reserve, the present moment. And all of a sudden I wake up. The contrast between the sumptuous setting in my dream and the miserable reality of the prison is overwhelming. When I realize where I am, I am seized with a boundless despair. Will I ever see my wife and my children again?

The day of Tuesday May 9th passes, in general, like the previous days. The only differences are in the meals. In the morning, instead of bacon fat, we are given three-fourths of a cup of warm water, labeled tea. It is true that it has a vague smell of lime and the warden pretends it also has sugar in it. If it has sugar, then it is so little that I cannot detect it. Also, the lunch and dinner are composed of barley, not beans. This barley meal, i.e. decorticated barley, the food of the poor regions where wheat doesn't grow, is obtained by boiling barley grains in water and adding some vegetables – carrots and onions -and some oil at the end. What results is not tasty, however it is food. But there are different kinds of barley meals: from the dense and thick – a sort of ordinary pilaf – with enough vegetables and oil and consequently a bearable taste, to the whitish juice, without or with very few vegetables and little oil, in which you find, on the bottom of the tin two spoonfuls of grains. While the former makes you feel full at least, the latter only deceives your hunger. In fact, even the wardens when – quite often – we happened to have barley of this kind, mockingly called it "tea". Unfortunately, for three years and two months, from May 8, 1950 to July 3, 1953 barley was the main meal in prison, and there were periods, like between December 20, 1950 and January 5, 1951[26] when we were given it all the time for lunch and dinner.

At about ten o'clock in the morning, the civilian from the first day appears. He holds a book in which he writes my last and first name, my birthday, my parents names and my last address. Then he asks me whether I kept some of the bread that was given to us for the journey. I answer that I have nothing because I gave a loaf and half of the second to my colleague N. Crețu when we left the van. At the end, he tells me that I am not allowed to look out of the window; in case I disobey this order "it will be very bad" for me.

---

[26] This period coincides with the winter holidays

I wonder why they forbid the prisoners to look out of the window. From the very way the windows are situated, six feet above the floor, it results that this interdiction is old and it existed during the Austrian-Hungarian monarchy. It is, of course, a consequence of the principle of *isolation* which combines with the principle of *reclusion*; the result is a complete separation from the social environment. The lack of communication with the other prisoners and, generally, with anybody apart from the prison staff, causes great suffering. I ascertain, from my own experience, the truth of the definition that the philosopher in olden times gave about human being: "Social animal". The contact with your kind becomes imperatively necessary; you resort to all kinds of means in order to see – for a moment – the face of a "fellow" or to be able to have a word with him.

What possibilities does the cell offer from this point of view? I begin by analyzing *the window* about which the civilian has warned me. If you climb on the edge of the bed, you can see the ground outside, so you can see those who walk or work in the yard. But you are seen in your turn, by the sentinel in the watch tower. There is one position in which the sentinel cannot see you: when you look through the right lower corner, staying near the edge of the window, close to the wall. You also can avoid being seen if you look through the middle of the window, but staying in the center of the cell, or at least five feet away from the window. In both cases the danger is of being seen, *through the observation hole*, by the wardens who patrol in the hall. Therefore, before climbing on the bed in order to look out the window, you have to make certain that nobody is in the hall near your cell. And even so, you only can look for a few seconds because, meanwhile, it's very possible that one of the agents can come near your cell and look through the observation hole. I consider the *door* of the cell now. I immediately notice that the "vasisdas" [27] is not perfectly closed on its' hinges. Between the hinge and the edge of the opening there is, at some places, a 1 to 1 1/2 millimeter space. I try to see whether this space can be enlarged. I try to push the shutter with the end of the spoon. After many attempts, I get a very small shift; now there is a crack 2 millimeters wide and 10 long, which allows me to see what happens in the hall near my cell. Thus, before climbing on the bed, I look through this crack to see whether someone spies

---

[27] The rectangular opening in the door.

near my cell. I repeat this operation every five or six seconds. It is true that, not having my glasses, I don't see clearly, and I can't distinguish faces at twelve feet away; the important thing is that I see whether there is someone in uniform, an enemy, in the hall. I am also favored by the fact that my hearing is still good, maybe to compensate for the bad sight. I can hear the slightest move, in the hall or in the yard, even when someone walks in felt shoes; this fact helped me many times not to be caught red-handed when I broke regulations.

Today's warden is an unlikable guy, with cold snake-like eyes; he walks bowleggedly; I found out later, still because of the carelessness of his colleagues who called him by name, that his name is Arba. My friends from inmate group seventeen told me, two years later, that this man spent many years in prison for homicide and that the present regime released him. Therefore he was the right man to make a communist and a trustee and to be made to watch the former ministers of the previous regime.

The sun enters my cell at about half past ten-eleven and leaves it at about three in the afternoon. A band of light, rather narrow, which shows up at the beginning on the western wall, goes down to the floor and then goes up onto the eastern wall and, eventually, it disappears. It is sufficient, however, for me to have some sun. I move my bed so that the light falls on it and I take a kind of sun-bath.

I keep pacing thousands of steps in the cell, from the door to the window and back. For reasons of health, I make the decision to do such a march daily and to divide it into three parts: a part in the morning, before lunch, another part in the afternoon, between four and five and a third part after dinner, before I go to bed. I remember the English proverb: "After luncheon rest a while, after dinner walk a mile"; and I have decided to apply it. I will also do some exercises after I wake up and before I wash myself. Washing is a problem: you have to get accustomed to having only two cups of water which you are given in the morning, between five and half past five. I have a piece of good toilet soap – Turkish soap, "Dephne" – but I have to use it sparingly, so that I have it for as long as I can; god knows how long we will stay here! Also, I have to take care of my clothes, underwear and shoes so that I don't end up wearing rags. I don't want to have happen to me what happened to Constantinescu-Iaşi, who, when he got out of Doftana penitentiary, after one year and seven months of detention, had no shoes. Al. Alexandrini told me that when he was imprisoned, at the Ministry of the Interior, he found in his cell a police officer -a prisoner himself – who advised him to take care of his clothes, to wear only his shirt and long underwear as much as he could, because otherwise they would be worn out in a short time; of course, the officer was wearing himself only a shirt and long underwear.

The third night in the prison begins with an incident that deeply troubles all the prisoners. It is one hour after "lights out" and I am sleeping when a gunshot awakens me suddenly. At the same time, I hear the desperate cry of the sentinel: "Halt, or I'll shoot!" and new gunfire. "The alarm" is always given by repeated banging on a piece of iron which is placed on the watch tower, near the sentinel. The prison wardens, armed, cross the hall at a run and go out into the yard. At this moment a siren begins to wail in the night, reminding us of the times of aerial bombardments. The idea crosses my mind that it is a set-up, an arranged fight, someone simulating an attack upon the prison, in order to have a pretext for shooting all of us. I remember having read in the volumes "On the edge of the Precipice" how the ministers and the other dignitaries imprisoned in Jilava were executed by the fascists. I see in my mind a photograph in which one of the fascists – Sîrbu, if my memory isn't wrong – shoots through the half opened doors of the cells with a revolver. And I expect, at any moment, for the door of my cell to open. I have nothing to defend myself with; but I would like, if possible, not to die before I hit my attacker in the head. I take my suitcase and post myself to the left of the door standing with my back to the wall. The attacker cannot see me if he only opens the door, so he can't shoot from outside; he must step inside. This step is enough for me to give him a strong smack in the head with the suitcase and try to snatch the revolver out of his hand. I realize that, eventually, the result is the same: I will be undoubtedly killed but I don't want to die like that; before dying I want to kill one or even many of these beasts. I hear a long, muffled rustling throughout the entire prison; the prisoners are all awake and think, I am sure, the same way as I do: that they want to "wipe us out".

Time passes and the cell door doesn't open; the siren falls silent – it was a factory siren announcing the night shift, at ten o'clock – the wardens re-enter the prison at ease and peace is restored. The rustling in the cells calms down; the prisoners go to bed. I can only fall asleep after about an hour.

The following day – May 10 – is the first visit of the doctor. Immediately after the morning "tea" – the same warm yellowish water, with a slight lime smell – the door opens and a short man wearing glasses and the unavoidable cap – the sign of recognition for a real "democrat" – enters the cell. By his face, he seems to be a Jew. He takes two steps in the cell and stopping in front of me, his hands in his pockets, he says: "I am the doctor". "Glad to meet you" I answer "I am Professor Giurescu". "Do you suffer from something, did you come with an ailment from home?" – I reproduce textual his words. "I have nothing, with the exception of a twinge in my right shoulder blade, I contracted this twinge here, sleeping by the broken window the first night I came here". "All right, we will see" he answers; he turns on his heels and, without a good-bye or any word at all, he goes out. During this entire scene, the warden stayed by the open door, in order for the doctor to not be alone, even for a few seconds, with a prisoner. Suspicion and mutual fear are only two of the fundamental principles of the regime.

I have to keep track of the passing days; otherwise I risk after a while, not knowing the day and month we are in, not realizing when it is Sunday or a holiday. Thus, I decide to draw for each day, a short line on the door; actually I scratch, with a piece of glass, in the thick paint that covers the metal on the door and if possible, even on the metal itself. The first scratch represents the day of May 7, 1950, the date of my arrival in Sighet; then I draw three other scratches for the days of 8, 9, and 10.

The Sundays will be marked with a scratch which is longer and notched to the lower left. In order to mark the days when I receive news or when an event takes place, I use different scratches: longer scratches notched to the upper right or ending, at their upper extremity, with spirals.

Every morning, after I wash myself and before the roll call, I draw the appropriate scratch on the door of cell 21; I continue doing that with regularity up to and including January 25, 1952, when I am removed from "isolation" and placed in the inmates group Cornățeanu.

Two days later, on May 12, I receive a visit from the doctor again. I have nothing new to report: when I remind him about my twinge in the right shoulder blade, he only says what he said the first time, "We will see". The entire visit lasts twenty seconds. The next day, May

13, at around nine in the morning, a warden enters the cell and tells me to take my luggage and follow him. I wonder what it can be: release? Not very likely; is he moving me to another place? Is he taking me to an interrogation? But, in the latter case, why do I have to take the luggage? I make all kinds of assumptions, with the exception of the right one. We go to the end of the hall, then turn to the right, ascend the rocky stairs to the next floor and arrive next to a room where I see, sitting at a table, the civilian who gave out, that first morning, the breakfast; next to him, there is an under officer, short and with a dark complexion: he seems to be a warrant officer or a chief petty officer.

The walls of the room are provided with shelves on which rest all kinds of effects: clothes and underwear. I cannot distinguish well what sort of clothes, because I don't have my glasses: they remained at the Ministry of the Interior. The civilian tells me to put down the suitcase and to take off all of my clothes. I look at him with surprise: what does he want? He repeats the order, explaining at the same time: "We will give you other clothes and underwear." he hands me a short sleeved shirt and a pair of long underwear, both military issue, made of ordinary cotton. After that he takes a pair of pants and tells me: "Try these on". They are gray striped pants, a dark stripe followed by a light stripe: the prisoners uniform.

I protest energetically against the fact that I am given such a uniform before being judged and sentenced; addressing the civilian, I call him: Mister Superintendent. "I am the director of the prison, I am not a Superintendent", he answers angrily, adding: "As for the uniform, it spares your civilian clothes; when you get out of here, it's good for you to have your own clothes in good condition". However I continue to protest; the director tells me "I'm not following my own ideas; I got, from higher up, an order; I think it's better for you not to oppose it". I understand what is behind his words; I realize that my resistance will only lead to all kinds of "trouble". A clear understanding of the climate of the prison is revealed to me this morning when I hear the second floor warden shouting at one of the prisoners: "So what if you were a general? You're nothing now! Move faster when I tell you, otherwise I will slap your eyes out of your head, damn you, son of a bitch!"

I try the pants on; they are very tight around the waist, and the two upper buttons cannot be buttoned; I tell this to the director who placidly answers: "don't worry, they will fit you in two weeks; they will be just right". The truth is that, in two weeks, the pants fit me and after two months I had to take them in, to make them tighter because they were so large that they fell off of me. After the pants he gives me a jacket and a cap: the jacket is tight too, but the cap is too big. All the effects are worn out; they were worn by other prisoners before me.

When I see myself dressed like this, I have for a moment a terrible feeling of decay. I remember a convoy of prisoners that I saw passing on Berzei Street when I was a child; some of them had heavy chains on their feet, making a frightening noise. If someone saw me dressed like this and didn't know who I was, he would believe he had a prisoner in front of him, a killer. This humiliating state of mind only lasts for seconds; I recover; fortunately, I am able to control myself and the other two do not notice what happens in my soul. Later, the fellows in inmate group 18 tell me that they had had a real shock when they saw Burilleanu, the former governor of the National Bank, coming out of the effects room dressed in his new clothes.

The problem is not only the uniform; the fact that they dress us like this means that the detention will be longer, that it's not only a short-term one. This conclusion is more depressing.

After I dress myself, the director begins to make an inventory of the things in my suitcase; he writes a receipt. He doesn't allow me to take either of the two sweaters, or the towel – because of their dimension I could use them to hang myself – or the slippers; he also takes all of my underwear, I only keep a handkerchief and two pairs of socks. In exchange, he gives me another shirt and a pair of long underwear and a small napkin. Thus, I will have two sets of underwear: one on me and one to spare. He keeps my coat and my suitcase; also my comb and my beret. Of my toiletries I can only keep the toothbrush, a tube of tooth-paste and the soap; the razor and the packet of ten new Gillette blades they had taken away from me before, at the Ministry of the Interior. When he finishes the inventory of all the kept objects the director invites me to sign the receipt. I read it carefully and sign it; then the director makes a motion to the warden to take me back into my cell.

For lunch there's barley again; at dinner, the same barley but less dense, "barley soup", in reality a sort of leftover dish water. During the first week we only had barley and beans and for dinner we always had the same kind of food as for lunch, but worse, sometimes much worse. From the third day of detention in Sighet I begin to be hungry; I suffer from an almost permanent hunger which, eventually, becomes an obsession. A half an hour after you finish your lunch, you are hungry again; this sensation becomes more and more intense and grows to its fullest at half past five in the evening when, usually, the bell for dinner rings. After the watery soup in the evening you don't even have a half an hour respite like with lunch; you are hungry the moment you finish eating.

On May 20, on St. Constantin's Eve, I was shaved. A warden with the appearance of a mongoloid – some of the fellows nick-named him "mongoloid" – having pustules on his face and smelling heavily – I think he hadn't taken a bath for months – soaped my face and started to shave me. He wasn't a professional and, to be frank, I was very afraid that the straight-razor would go deeper than was necessary. I manage to stay safe throughout this, I only had about ten superficial cuts on my face and, because of the quality of the shaving, I appreciated the fact that two weeks after that I wasn't shaved anymore.

On the same day, May 20 – if my memory serves me – I received my first piece of "meat". Fifteen minutes before lunch, the cell door opened violently, as usual, and the warden on duty called: "Come and get meat". I came with my tin and the man, stabbing a fork into the bucket he had in his other hand, pulled out a bone with a little meat, skin and gristle on it – around 40-50 grams (ca. 1.4 – 1.6 oz) – and handed it to me. I was able to get about 10-15 grams of meat off of it. After that came "soup", in reality a very diluted broth in which I found two teaspoonfuls of barley.

I kindly ask the reader to believe that I am presenting the facts exactly as they were, without any alteration. I want to leave, about the time I spent in Sighet, "an objective document", I want to be as objective a man can be. I do not have in view either literary ends or political propaganda; I only want to make an honest testimony, to present the *truth*, to describe facts *as they happened*, in order that my contemporaries and those to come know what happened; it's up to them to make value judgments.

May 21st is the day of Saints Constantin and Elena: it's a sad anniversary for me. I was thinking of my oldest son, Dinu, who also had his name day today. What is he doing now? He graduated from the Faculty of Letters, specializing in History, in June of 1949 and he was supposed – together with his colleagues – to present his graduation thesis in the same month. He prepared as a graduation thesis the work "Costache Negri and the secularization of the monastery's' assets", showing, based on unpublished documents from the Romanian Academy – the Cuza Vodă archive – and from other sources, the important role that this statesman played in solving the ticklish and important problem of the secularization of the assets of the dedicated monasteries. To the surprise of all those who graduated that year, they were not allowed to present their graduate thesis' because the Ministry of Education – in fact the communist party – wanted to change this last exam according to the new ideology and the new organization of higher education. In autumn, the situation was the same: the party was still thinking about how to make the changes. In February of 1950 – by tradition those who had graduated the previous year were allowed to take the graduation exam in February – the situation was still the same. Seeing that there was no way for him to take this exam and in order not to waste time, he began, as soon as July of 1949, to prepare his Ph.D. thesis on "The life and achievements of Costache Negri". The work was to be based on the 263 unpublished letters addressed to Cuza Vodă which were in the Cuza Vodă archives at the Romanian Academy. He had copied all these letters and started to gather the rest of the materials. Because of the uncertain situation, in spring of 1950, he attended and graduated in first place from the courses of a school for foremen. At the end of April he was appointed foreman in a road construction company and he left for Andrășești where his job was.

He had been working for two weeks when, in May of 1950, the Ministry announced that the graduation exam was set for July. I sent the news to him, to the building site; he was supposed to come home on Saturday, May 6, and talk with me about the exam, but on Saturday morning I was arrested. I keep wondering now, here in prison, whether he will be able to prepare his exam while working as a foreman or if he will have to quit his job. And then, after he passes the exam, I wonder whether he will find a position which will permit him to commit himself to scientific research. In the previous year many of his colleagues were appointed into such positions; for him, because of the name he bears, this thing was not possible. The criteria for appointment was not the ranking of grades – as would be normal – but the social provenance and the affiliation with the communist party and its offshoots. He was asked by his colleague Malița, leader of the student organization, to join the party and he refused. The consequence was that instead of working in the field of Romanian history, for which he had a strong inclination and the necessary education, he now had to schedule work for men constructing roads in Bărăgan. He worked as a foreman, then as a head foreman, for many years – from 1950 to 1955 – without being able to do what he wanted to do. In June of 1950, when my family had to leave the house in two hours, he saw confiscated not only his library – together with mine – but also all of his research notes, including the copies of Negri's letters. All these materials, together with my research notes and the manuscripts of several articles that I had ready for printing, *were burned* in the yard of our house in Berzei Street by the vandals led by the famous Weber, the man who sent my family away.

I mention the case of my son only for its' representative value. This is one of the thousands of cases of young people from all over the country who saw their normal careers hindered by those who claimed to be the supporters and promoters of scientific research. As in many other fields, the practice didn't follow the theory. One didn't take into account the *personal value* of the young man who wanted to dedicate himself to a scientific or other activity, value proved by the marks gotten in exams taken, but instead other criteria such as social provenance, affiliation with the party or the services brought to the secret police by informing on his fellows, were considered.

Any parent whose children were in the same situation would understand me, and the thoughts that racked my brain that day of Saint Constantin, my sons' name day.

The next day, May 22, in the morning, I am taken "for the walk". It consists of thirty steps forward and thirty steps backward along the wall of the prison, in the big yard or in the small one. Before exiting the cell, the warden makes the necessary recommendations, according to the regulations: "hands must stay behind the back; head down". So, you are not allowed to look up at the sky, straight in front of you or to the side; the eyes should look permanently at the ground. The warden adds: "Don't dare to look at the windows, otherwise you are going to finish in 'Neagra'!" (the black cell)

"Neagra" is a cell without windows in which are closed, wearing only a shirt and underwear or even completely naked, those who break the regulations or upset the "bosses" in any way, i.e. the wardens and the other officials of the prison.

When I take the thirty steps forward and back I am subject to a double supervision: on one side the warden, on the other the sentinel; the former stays in the yard, the latter is up in the watch tower. Any attempt to cast your eyes upward, to the two upper floors, provokes the yells and sometimes references to your mother from the two men. It is easy for anyone to imagine how agreeable such a "walk" can be; however the conditions are, it is necessary because it gives you the possibility to breathe, for fifteen minutes, cleaner air. Besides, it is a variation in the exasperatingly monotonous and brutalizing life in the cell and also a distraction of your thoughts.

Moving along the wall of the prison, I observe the small windows of the basement. There are five windows. In a moment when the warden has his back turned to me I cast my eyes to the windows of the two upper floors; I cannot distinguish anything because I don't have my glasses. Nevertheless I have to find a way to find out who else is here, who my suffering "fellows" are. The occasion for that comes much sooner than I expected. Two minutes after I return to my cell, I hear voices outside in the yard, right next to my window. One of the voices is known to me; it seems to be Victor Papacostea's voice. I have to check this; I reassure myself that there is nobody in the hall to look through the observation opening and then I rush to the window; I get up on the edge of the bed and look through the upper right corner of the window, so that I cannot be seen by the sentinel. I see a group of around six or seven prisoners, all wearing the striped uniform, who chop wood right under my window. I force myself to distinguish the faces; I only have a few seconds for that, because meanwhile, someone can come into the hall and take me by surprise. I don't distinguish very much; I see the faces as if through a mist; however, I think I recognize Papacostea's' face. I go back to the door and look through the small crack: there is nobody; I go back to the window but, it's obvious, I cannot distinguish the faces. But I hear again the known voice and, this time, there is not a doubt: this is Papacostea.

Now, I have a sure way of communication with the others; through him I will find out the names of my colleagues in his group and the names of those with whom he arrived in the van from Bucharest. But he must know I am here, he must spot my cell. I check again at the door and getting up, for the third time, at the window I call his name. He turns his head to me for a moment; I think that he recognizes me too; he doesn't say anything because the warden and the sentinel keep their eyes on them, the wood-choppers.

It doesn't matter; we will have an opportunity to exchange a few words over the next few days.

A short time before lunch, the wood-choppers team returns to the building; we are given the food – the eternal barley – and an hour after that the "walks" begin. This time, it's only one man; he passes at about three feet from my window. I try to make out his face; I have the impression that this is Georges Strat. I call his name in a low voice, making an attempt; I call him a second time, a bit louder and exactly when he is under my window; this time, he slightly turns his head to me. As the lower part of my face is covered by the edge of the window – he only can see my eyes – I say my name. He nods slightly: he understood.

So, this is the second way of communication with the others. Like this, within a few weeks, I manage to recognize a series of people, to get in touch with them and to find out through them the names of the other prisoners.

Dumitru Alimănișteanu who is also alone in his cell, but on the third floor – the first cell after the corner – tells me that he saw Gen. Artur Văitoianu, who can hardly walk; it is true that he had some problems with his legs for the past three years, from 1947 on. He also saw the brothers Lapedatu – Ion and Alexandru – Constantin Argetoianu, Radu Roșculeț and August Filip. With the latter two I had the chance to speak during the "walks"; Roșculeț told me that he saw Vasile Sassu.

A couple of men that I recognize easily are Ștefan Meteș and Silviu Dragomir; they are in the same cell and go on their walk together. Silviu Dragomir walks in the front; six feet behind him, according to the regulations, walks Meteș. Dragomir has lost a lot of weight; he had already served a year and a half in prison – for a non-political reason – at the moment we were arrested; he was brought here from Caransebeș where Dr. Costinescu was also imprisoned.

By the beginning of July, while I am taking the thirty steps forward and back along the wall of the prison, I suddenly see at one of the small windows of the basement a sympathetic face with expressive and lively eyes and I clearly hear the words: "Who are you?" On my way back he repeats the question; I realize he must be one of my fellow sufferers, who is animated by the same need to find out the names of the others; so I tell him my name in a low voice. Neither the warden nor the sentinel notice anything. When I pass for the third time, he asks another question: "What cell are you in?" I whisper: "Cell number 21 on the first floor!" He shakes his head, signaling he understands, and tells me: "We are a group of Uniate priests."

This is the first contact with this group. The one who approached me is priest Rațiu from Timișoara. I found this out later, from his own mouth, on the occasion of one of the numerous "conversations" – each during a few seconds – that we had.

The following day, I hear voices in the yard; I look out of the window and see two young people in black clothes, in direct view of the window; one of them asks the other: "Have you read Professor Giurescu's' History?" they want to tell me, in this way, that yesterday during my walk, they caught my name and the number of my cell. I wave my hand at them and they bow slightly. After several minutes, they come even closer to the window and, talking between them loud enough for me to hear perfectly, they say: "Here there are four bishops and twenty-one Uniate priests". Then, probably fearing I didn't hear them, they repeat it: "So, as I said, here there are four bishops and twenty-one Uniate priests". I answer: "I understand; please give my regards to them all".

In the same afternoon, I have the chance to see the bishops. I hear voices of elderly people in the yard. I look out of the window and see around ten prisoners walking in a circle, one after the other, keeping their hands behind their backs. Among them, there are two bearded old men; the others, young and elderly, are shaven; they all wear black clothes, clergy-like. I suppose that the bishops must be in this group. I greet them by bowing; two of them, those who are directly in view of the window, nod in return; another two salute with a hand to their temples. Three days later, when the same group is in the yard again, for the "walk", I repeat my greeting; in answer to my greeting, one of the elderly clergymen asks me: "Who are you?" I say my name; he stares at me and I understand that he didn't hear me; I repeat it and he shakes his head that he doesn't understand.

I am not surprised; during the two months that have passed since my arrest, I've grown so thin that I am unrecognizable; in addition to this I don't have my glasses on. Seeing that my third attempt fails – it is true that I cannot speak loud because I am afraid of being heard by one of the wardens in the hall, and the group of bishops is rather far from my window, about fifteen to twenty feet – I decide to try another way. I have a big piece of paper in my cell, originating from a cement bag, that I found one morning near the toilets. I cut my name out of the paper, with great difficulty, using a sliver of glass; the letters are about 2.5 inches high and can be seen from where the bishops are. I need three hours to complete this task; I am careful all the time not to be seen through the opening by one of the agents in the hall. After I finish, I hide the piece of paper in the straw of my pillow; I have to wait two days until their new walk. If the paper is found by a warden, the result will be enormous; it is against what the administration wants to ensure to the highest degree, "the secret", i.e. the lack of any contact between prisoners, the prevention of any communication between them. That is why we are not allowed to look out of the window, that is why we mustn't know who is in the other cells, that is why the isolation is complete.

Fortunately, nobody checks me and there is no search in these two days.

When the bishops are in the yard again, after we greet each other, which is a ritual now, I raise the paper above my head so that it can be seen by those who walk in the yard. On the first attempt they can't read it; I raise it a bit higher and, this time, I see that they understand; two of them nod. One of these, the tallest, makes a questioning movement with his head and quickly draws circles in the air in front of his eyes; i.e.: where are my glasses? I make a sign with my hand to indicate a long distance; they remained at the Ministry of the Interior in Bucharest.

I had found out from the priests, before, the names of the bishops; His Holiness Hossu is easier to recognize, he has a distinctive face. The others are: Bishop Frenţiu – he will die here in prison, in Sighet – and Bishop Russu. I cannot see Bishop Suciu; I will find out later that he suffers from a serious stomach illness; he will also die in Sighet on June 26 or 27, 1953.

Among the Uniate clergymen, in the bishops' group was the canon Macovei; among those in the bishops' group I am impressed by Father's Brânzeu Brânzeu physical appearance; well built, strong, wearing a big beard, he almost always walks in front of the others; one day, I hear his Holiness Hossu saying about him that he is 74 years old; despite his age, he holds up very well.

The description of the prison.
The building

Before describing the way of life in the Sighet prison and the most important facts about what happened there, I think it is necessary that I make a detailed description of this institution, i.e. the building, the staff and the regulations. This is the physical and psychological framework within which our lives will develop for five years and two months and without knowing it, the reader cannot follow and understand fully what happened.

"The main penitentiary" in Sighet was built by the Hungarians in 1896, on the occasion of the celebration of a "thousand years" of Hungarian rule here (896 – 1896); at the same time a series of other public buildings were built in Transylvania as well as in the rest of Hungary. Maybe it would have been better if they had built a school, a theater or a hospital here; but they built a prison. The building was imposing in its' proportions: the ground floor and two upper floors – around forty-eight feet high – occupied a rectangle bordered on all sides by streets. The walls are thick, the material is of high quality, and the workmanship – as far as I can deduce from some details, for example, the woodwork in the attic, the arches in the cells, the floor of the catwalks on each floor – is very carefully done. This prison was considered, in the years of the Austrian-Hungarian monarchy, to be one of the most modern and rigorous prisons. The name 'Sighet' – together with that of Gherla – called up at that time the image of hard time prison. Indeed, the big number of individual cells in Sighet offered – and continues to offer today – the possibility of strict isolation for a large number of prisoners.

The building reserved for the political prisoners – that in which I stayed from 1950 to 1955 – is T-shaped; it is made up of a main body which is the base of the 'T', running from east to west, and the second section, representing the top of the 'T', running from north to south.

The base of the 'T' is not all the same width; at about half-way, it becomes two feet narrower on each side; consequently, the cells in the second half of the building are a bit smaller than those in the first half. As you enter the big hall – resembling the main nave of a gothic

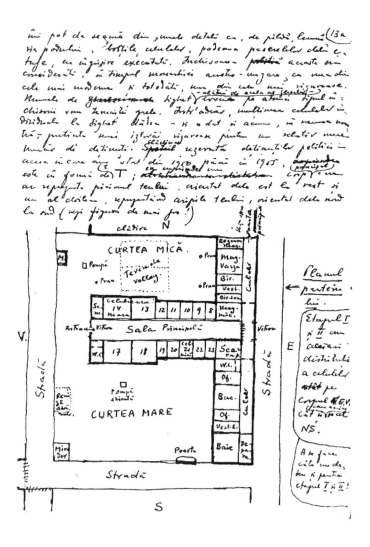

General plan of the Sighet Penitentiary – drawn by the author

cathedral – you see to your left the small rocky stairs leading on one side to the basement and on the other to the second and third floors. Further along, also on the left, there are two large cells – numbers thirteen and fourteen – and after these, one after the other, five small cells (numbers eight through twelve) and then "the small store" i.e. the room where the daily food supply is kept.

On the right, immediately next to the entrance, is the closet, proceeded by a vestibule, then on the left, two large cells – numbers seventeen and eighteen – and after these, there are five small cells (numbers nineteen through twenty-three) and, at the end, a large stone staircase which leads to the next floor.

The arrangement of the cells, on the side and then the large rooms, is, as one can see, symmetric. This room receives light through two large windows situated at the two ends, about three yards wide and nine yards high. In the windows there are pairs of window panes which can be opened and closed. The best cell on the floor is number seventeen, situated above the boiler room and having a wall getting heat from the boiler room chimney thus benefiting from the most heat in the winter; the worst cell is number twelve, situated where the base of the 'T' narrows, at a dead angle, with less light and more dampness. In this cell were Dinu Brătianu, in 1950, and Constantin Argetoianu in 1954-55.

The right wing of the 'T', looking in from the entrance, has a long corridor, at the end of which is the de-lousing room for the prisoners 'effects'. In this room is a boiler which feeds warm steam for the de-lousing room and heat to another boiler for the bathroom. To the right of the corridor, as you look at the de-lousing room, there are in order, the following: the toilet, preceded by a small entrance hall in which there is a tap, the kitchen with a pantry, and communicating between them – the pantry door to the corridor was bricked up and plastered over before we arrived – was a storage room which was converted, in 1953, into a second pantry, the bathroom vestibule and the bathroom. The kitchen and the bathroom are the same size as the big cells in the main hall; all of the other rooms are exactly the same size as the small cells.

The left wing of the 'T' has, like the right side, a long corridor at the end of which is the exit to the main gate of the prison. On the left of the corridor there are two offices separated by a hall, then a larger room with a cement floor, which serves for the storage of vegetables for daily use, pickled cabbage and pickles, and at the end a smaller

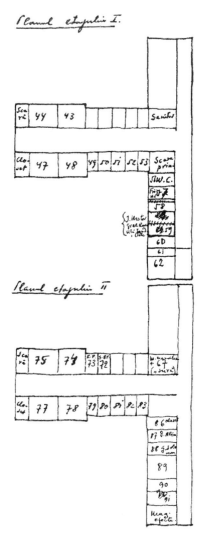

Plan of the 1st and 2nd floor of the Sighet Penitentiary
– drawn by the author

room, also with a cement floor and connected to the previous room, in which the barrel of cooking oil and the boxes of marmalade are kept. This room used to be a bathroom, having showers and a tap. The offices have roughly the same dimensions as two small cells; the vegetable storage room is as big as two large cells, the rest of the rooms are the size of a small cell. The small hall, the corridors, the toilets, the kitchen with the pantries and the bathroom vestibule are paved with grit stone plates; the bathroom has a cement floor.

The upper floors reproduce the division of the ground floor exactly in the case of the main body and approximately in the case of the 'T' wings. Thus, on the second floor, there are two large cells to the right of the main room (numbers forty-seven and forty-eight) and two on the left (numbers forty-four and forty-five), and ten small cells, five on the right (numbers forty-nine through fifty-three) and five on the left (numbers thirty-nine through forty-three). Cell number thirty-nine, the last on the left, is "Neagra" (the black cell).

On the right wing of the 'T', after the toilet, is the barbers room, the same size as a small cell, then two small cells, two large cells (numbers fifty-eight and fifty-nine), and again two small cells (numbers sixty and sixty-one) and, at the end, a big cell (number sixty-two) preceded by a vestibule. Now, on the left wing of the 'T' there is the medics room, where he keeps medicines and his paperwork, then a few small cells, a big cell which is as big as three small ones and, at the end of the corridor, the big room serving for storage. This room used to be the prison chapel; one could still see, in 1950, stars and other elements painted on the wall which indicated worship; the communists converted it into a storeroom for different things – beds, mattresses etc. – and beginning in 1955 it also served as a storeroom for prisoners belongings.

The best cells on the second floor were number fifty-nine, above the kitchen and thus having more warmth in winter, and number sixty-two, from where one could see (if one climbed on the bed) the street going south and a part of the hill to the south-east. This hill was covered with forests and orchards and, as Miluță Romașcanu told me, even a patch with grape vines. The worst cell on this floor was number forty-three, situated exactly above cell number twelve.

On the third floor, to the right of the main hall there are: the toilet, two big cells (number seventy-seven and seventy-eight) and five small cells (numbers seventy-nine through eighty-three); on the left is the stair going down to the lower floors, then again two big cells (numbers seventy-five and seventy-four) and five small cells (numbers sixty-nine through seventy-three).

The cell numbered sixty-nine is also called "Neagra" (the black cell) and it is exactly above the "Neagra" on the second floor.

The right wing of the 'T' reproduces the division of the same wing on the second floor exactly; the last cell together with its' vestibule – situated above cell number sixty-two – serves as the prisons' storage room for personal 'effects': the striped uniforms, the underwear, sheets, boots etc. are kept here; the naphthalene smell is piercing.

The left wing of the 'T' has, at its' beginning, a cell which, like the one underneath on the second floor, doesn't get the light *directly* from the yard, but through a small window, about a third of the size of a normal window, in the corridor; therefore they call this cell "Sura" (the gray room); it is a punishment cell because there isn't enough air and light. Ilie Lazăr was put here, for many months in 1953; when we carried the food in the tubs and arrived by the "Sura", he popped up, looking through the bars of the small window and communicating or asking for information.

After this cell come a series of small cells, then a big one which is used for storing food; here the bags of corn meal were kept, the beans, the barley and the salt all in large quantities; the "small store" on the ground floor was supplied from here. There is a big difference between the cells on the right and those on the left of the main hall, respectively to the south or to the north. The cells that are oriented to the south are well exposed to the sun; the suns' rays enter these cells for a few hours each day, in the morning and in the afternoon. In cell number twenty-two for example, there was sun for four hours a day; in autumn and winter, the suns' rays reached as far as the back of the cell, climbing on the door up to its' middle; in spring and summer the rays were shorter, the light band being just a narrow line in June. Those who stayed in this cell were able to take sunbathes and, in fact, many of the prisoners really did. On the other hand, the cells situated to the north, to the left of the main hall were badly placed; they *never* received the suns' rays. Twice I stayed in cell number ten, which is across from cell number twenty-one, the first time in winter, in December of 1950, the second time in summer, in June of 1951; I never saw a speck of light in the room. The suns' rays advance at maximum to the edge of the window in June, without entering the room. In autumn and winter they don't even reach the wall.

The basement, which one gets to by the small rocky stairs at the beginning of the main hall, is made up of: the wheel-pump room, the boiler room, the coal storeroom and two cellars. In the first cellar they used to keep carrots and in the second, potatoes.

At the beginning, in 1950, the coal storeroom was connected by a door, to the potato cellar; the latter one wasn't connected to the carrot cellar. The following year, the above mentioned door was bricked up and a new door was cut between the two cellars. The pump and boiler rooms and the coal storeroom get light through five small windows which look out on the big yard; the two cellars that look out on the small yard have four small windows.

These two yards are situated on both sides of the main body of the building, the big yard on its' right, as you look at the entrance door, and the small one on its' left.

In the big yard I found a hand pump which didn't work anymore at that time and a small barn made of wood, along the western wall of the premises, a barn that was abandoned later. In the southwestern corner of the yard, built upon a solid trunk of fir tree and supported by two walls of the premises, at about twenty feet high there was a watchtower, a shelter for the sentinel who supervised the windows of the prison as well as the yard. Initially one could get to this watchtower by a stairway which descended into the yard; later this stair was torn down, and the sentinel had access to the tower by an opening made in the wall of the neighboring house – this house belonged to the police as well – by following the top of the wall and taking a staircase descending into the yard of the neighboring house. All these arrangements were made in order to avoid the soldiers tram-ping through the yard of the prison, i.e. to avoid the possibility of any contact, direct or indirect, with the prisoners; so the "secret" is better ensured. Also they avoided the opening, every three hours, of the main prison gate (placed on the southern wall of the premises) and thus they avoided the possibility of prisoners escaping through the gate.

It is true that an escape through the main gate, during the changing of the sentinels, had almost no chance of success; but in order to cut any possibility they resorted to this measure. "Vigilance" was one of the main concerns of the staff of the prison; that explains a whole series of measures that were made successively, during the five years, to ensure the "secret" and preventing any attempts to escape.

In the small yard – this was about three-fifths the size of the large yard – there was a second watchtower, near the western wall of the premises, at about eighteen feet from the northwest corner of the yard. Here too, the change of sentinels was done, initially, by a wooden staircase which connected the yard with the tower; then this staircase was torn down too, and access was gained from the top of the premise wall like in the big yard. Near this second watchtower was a lilac bush, rather high; it was cut down in 1951 because it hindered the sight of the sentinel in a little part of his view of the small yard. It seems this was the same reason they cut off, initially the tops (in 1951) of two fir trees in the yard of the building on the other side of the street to the south, and then they cut down the fir trees completely. In this way they suppressed the only vegetation which the prisoners in the cells on the first floor looking at the big yard could feast their eyes on.

Near the lilac bush was a hand pump; a pipe ran from the well of this pump to the wheel-pump in the basement of the building. When the wheel-pump didn't work because its' sealing rings were worn out we pumped the water with the hand pump; and when this pump was out of order, we took water directly from the well with a bucket tied to a rope.

At half-way between the pump and the wall of the main body of the building there is a tree; when I arrived there, in 1950, it was very small and frail; in the summer of 1955 it had grown large.

In the back of the yard, near the wall on the left wing of the building, there were two big fruit trees. They bore fruit in all years but in 1951 and 1953 they bore large crops.

This small yard was bordered, with the exception of its' western side, by a hedge. This hedge used to grow every year to the height of two and a half feet; the leaves were dark green; the flowers – resembling marigolds – were the color of light purple, with yellow centers; they used to bloom in early autumn. I often cast my eyes upon these flowers; they symbolized for us all the gardens we had seen before, in freedom. At around the end of September or the beginning of October when the other flowers, in fields, died or withered, hundreds of bees crowded above the small purple corollas. At the western end of this hedge, near the wall of the building, were a few yellow lilies with long leaves, like the iris and with elegant but odorless flowers.

In 1952, in the center of the small yard, a volleyball court was established, exclusively for the prison staff. I often saw the wardens, wearing T-shirts and sport shoes, playing for hours. During the first two years, different vegetables, especially tomatoes and potatoes, were grown in the small yard; in 1951 a small area was seeded with poppies; the poppies had pinkish-blue flowers and large pods.

The two yards were connected by a corridor around twelve feet wide; in this corridor was an entrance door to the main body of the building.

The wall of the premises – thick and massive – was about twenty feet high. It was shorter before; then three or four feet more was added.

The Sighet penitentiary served, when northern Transylvania was occupied by the Russian army, as a Russian prison. Here were brought (Miluță Romașcanu told me) all kinds of Russian offenders, deserters and also those who were awaiting transfer to the Soviet Union.

On the door of the barbers room (cell number fifty-seven), on the second floor, I read the following writing: "Serebriacov (?) sedil zdes" which means "Serebriacov was here". (I am not sure about the name!). Next to this writing was drawn, with talent, a dancing ballerina; the movement of her dress is done with great craftsmanship.

Miluță Romașcanu also told me that he saw bloodstains and traces of bullets on the walls and the floor of a cell. On the wall facing the big yard of the prison there were quite visible, when we came in May of 1950, two drawn faces of Russian soldiers, like those that are usually used as targets, at shooting practice.

On the door of cell number ten, on the ground floor, I read some writing in Romanian by someone called Gherghei which said "Scrişi lu", which is the old form of the verb "scrisei" (I wrote). When I arrived in Sighet, the building was in a state of neglect. The heater didn't work any longer, and probably hadn't for a long while; in a series of cells there weren't light bulbs anymore; in the main hall, where the light was switched on and off, the light switches were missing. The toilets were in a terrible state; no flushing. Near the bathroom, kitchen and toilets the mildew flourished high on the walls. The outer walls of the prison had not been painted for a long time; the cells were dirty, the floor had rotted boards; window panes were missing.

The renovation began in July, starting with the plumbing system, the bathroom and the toilets. The workers who were doing this were Hungarian, I heard them speaking Hungarian all day long. It would have been a good opportunity to correct some of the failings of the old plumbing; for example, the kitchen had no drainage pipe and the tap didn't work well, not giving enough water. Some of the toilets had no drainage grates to allow drainage of water collected from the taps and from emptied tubs of feces. So in the morning after emptying and cleaning the containers of feces and taking water in the mess tins, we would find the floor covered with 1-2 centimeter layer of liquid; we had to take this liquid with a dustpan or with rags, and put it into the holes of the "Turkish chairs"; if such drainage grates existed, this entire repulsive and unhygienic operation could be avoided.

We had the same problem with the wheel-pump in the basement. Because of the worn out sealing rings, the water gushed out around the piston and collected on the floor; because there was not drainage, in a short time the cement floor was covered with water; the "firemen" had permanently wet boots and cold feet. When there was too much water on the floor, it was put into a tub and carried up the stairs to be emptied in the toilet on the ground floor. None of these failings were corrected when the repairs happened; Was it inability or was it bad will? Was it lack of practical spirit or rather the desire to impose even harder work and more disgusting chores, to humiliate, in this way too, the representatives of the former leading class? Whatever the answer is, those who were in charge of this are to be blamed.

After they finished with the water system, the missing panes of glass were replaced and in September the electric system was repaired. There were powerful light bulbs installed that stayed on all night. It's very easy for anybody to imagine how we slept under these conditions. Especially those who were used to sleeping in complete darkness found it hard to close their eyes in the beginning. All the requests we made in order for the light to be turned off for the night received the same answer: "It's not possible". I understood later, after I was moved into a group, that this measure was an extra punishment for those who were alone in cells; in inmate groups, especially those who worked, the lights were often turned off during the night. All we could get, after a month of persistence, was to have the powerful bulb replaced with a less powerful one.

The operation that took the longest time was the repair of the central heating system. It began in late summer of 1950 and lasted, with interruptions, until spring of 1951. Thus, in the first winter of our stay, we used wood stoves. They had to replace the old boiler system, much too small for such a building, with a new bigger one. All the pipes were checked and reinstalled, and an electric pump was installed to propel warm water successively to different parts of the prison. This last operation used to be done with the help of faucets that opened and closed the warm water access to different parts of the installation. The large pipes that carried the warm water from the boiler were insulated with asbestos. The heating system worked well during the first two winters; after that, a water leak happened in the interior of the boiler so that an important repair was necessary. To this end they brought a group of welders from another town, probably Satu Mare.

Plan of a wing of the Sighet Penitentiary
– drawn by the author

The prison's staff

The main penitentiary in Sighet had, between 1950 – 1955, numerous staff. I had the impression, judging from the large number of faces that I saw here, that no other prison in the country had such a large staff to prisoner ratio. There were periods when the staff was as high as a third of the number of prisoners; and there was a point where it reached as much as two-fifths. For a few months in 1953 the staff was greatly reduced, there was a small number of wardens, so small that it was hard for them to cope with the requirements of their job; after this short period their numbers increased rapidly. During the last year, I observed especially that the number of officers increased; there was a certain time in April of 1955 when we had not less than five, namely: the director with a rank of Lieutenant-Major; his deputy director, a Lieutenant; two duty officers, both Sub-Lieutenants; and the "security" officer, a Lieutenant-Major.

As for the wardens, there generally were two of them for each "section" – the ground floor, the second floor and the third floor – with each floor being a section; therefore, usually they were called "section heads" instead of wardens.

There was a period when we had three heads for each section, changing every eight hours, which makes nine of them for each section and twenty-seven total. We also had times when there was only one section head and only two shifts per day, of twelve hours each. But usually, during the main part of the five years and two months, we had two section heads per section and two shifts per day. The first shift began at seven in the morning, the second at seven at night.

We can classify the four categories of staff at Sighet penitentiary: *Administrative Staff*, made up of the director, deputy-director (only in the first months!), duty officer, wardens and superintendents, and the accountant and his subordinates; the *Medical Staff*, made up of a doctor and a hospital attendant; the *Security Staff*, represented by only one officer; and the *Military Guard Staff*, i.e. the sentinels, the enlisted men who assisted with the change of the sentinels, and the officers who commanded the military detachments.

I will present, one after the other, each category, describing the people I came into contact with; when the information comes from my fellows, I will always specify so.

The director

I mentioned before in this book the circumstances under which I discovered who the director was. At this point, I had the chance to observe him during the next five years, in different situations, states of mind and conjunctures. I present further the results of this observation.

Of medium height, thin with a swarthy face, with a penetrating gaze, Vasile Ciolpan "I found out his name from my fellows in inmate group seventeen" was born in Transylvania. The way he used to speak, using regional words and expressions – he used to say, for example, "cioante" (from the Hungarian "csont") instead of "oase" (the Romanian word for "bones"), "nu-i baiu" (for "it doesn't matter"), "lucră" (for "he works") etc., – did not allow any doubt about it. It seems that he was from the northern part of Transylvania, maybe even from Maramureş; or at least this is what some of my fellows affirmed and I tend to believe that they were right. When he was young, the same fellows said, he was a wood-cutter in the forest; it is certain that he was an expert in issues connected with cutting, chopping and stacking of wood; many times he taught us how to stack the wood in the big yard. He told me, in the summer of 1950, that he had fought on the eastern front and he spent many years as a prisoner in the Soviet Union. Two weeks after he was taken prisoner, be-fore arriving in a camp, he starved terribly, eating only raw cabbage hearts and pumpkins, without any bread. (He told me that in response to my complaint that the food we were given at that time was of a miserable quality and insufficient.) He had missed his wife and children, he said he had four children at home, and had wondered whether he would ever return to his country; as he realized later that these thoughts were diminishing his capacity for resistance, he decided not to think of his family any longer and to wait, concentrating on his daily life. "If I return, what will be, will be; I will see at that time". This was the response to my repeated observations that I had no news about the family that I had left behind. The directors' intentions were not bad, only his recipe wasn't applicable to me; it supposes a certain temperament and a certain concept of life that I did not have.

He wasn't very educated; I think he only had had four years of grade school; but he had a natural intelligence which helped him to give, very often, appropriate remarks, sometimes even surprising ones. He spoke some Hungarian and a little bit of Russian. None of the prison staff spoke any western language; therefore, we would very often speak French when we were in the cells or in the yard; still in French – sometimes also in Italian or Latin – we received information from the Uniate priests, "the boys," as we used to call them.

Vasile Ciolpan, nicknamed by us "P.H.", did not have good health; he was suffering from a liver ailment; he told that to Gen. Nae Marinescu, with whom he used to talk sometimes. His face often looked bad, with sunken and emaciated cheeks. When, after July of 1953, the food became better and some of the fellows began to look better, their faces filling out, he used to make (with envy, or in the best of cases with melancholy) comparisons between the way he looked and the way they looked. We saw him, many times, with boils on his neck or on his temples; "With those his bad character is shown" the fellows asserted, jokingly. Maybe it was because of his precarious health or because of his drinking. He liked to drink; numerous times we saw him tipsy at the roll call, in the evening, and sometimes at noon too. In such situations he was, generally, in a good mood; he used to say a nice word or make a promise which of course he didn't remember the next day. Only once did I see him tipsy and furious: it was in 1953, in the spring, during the Korean war. There were, probably, serious bombardments of Korea by the Americans when, meeting us in the hall (I was bringing some coal for the kitchen in from the yard, with a fellow) he stopped us and, with a congested face, eyes red from drink and with slurred speech told us out of the blue: "Eat, countries! Drink, cities!". We didn't understand his words; when we asked him what he meant by this, he repeated the phrase and then motioned for us to go. Later, when we discussed this puzzling phrase with the fellows in the cell, we made the connection to the events in Korea – "the boys" and a friendly warden had told us about the terrible bombardments there and of the fact that here the communists were worried that the war would start in Europe too – and thus explained the meaning of the phrase.

He took his authority very seriously; when he gave an order he expected it to be obeyed immediately. He wasn't impressed by the inspections of the prison and didn't bow in front of higher ranked officers. "This one doesn't give orders to me" he said one day in the kitchen speaking of a Captain, who obviously had a higher rank, who came to inspect the prison. He probably felt he had a solid party position, because of his personal position and from the connections he had made as well. It seems that he was an old communist, in any case from before the war against the Soviet Union. He often hinted at the time he spent in prison and the way he was treated by the bourgeois regime. Was it true what he said? Or was it a simple standard phrase, intended to be a response to our complaints regarding the very tough regime – from the psychological point of view especially – to which we were subjected? In any case, he was "a trustworthy man", since the party entrusted him to control the prison which contained the majority of the former leaders of the country. He used to expound upon the communist doctrine – of course, as much as his cultural level could allow – and the communist methods. One day when, exasperated with suffering, one of the fellows told him: "You better shoot us", he responded: "We, the communists, do not kill, we have our methods to bring you to despair."

What he said was true about Sighet: the prisoners killed themselves out of despair, they perished because of diseases and lack of medical care, they became insane. I believe there is no other prison in the country which had such a large percentage of deaths, suicides and insanity.

He generally knew how to control his temper. But, from time to time, he had outbursts revealing his true nature, the depths of his violence. When Aurelian Bentoiu was brought from Bucharest ill, by train, the director together with several wardens were waiting for him in order to pick him up. Bentoiu told them that, being very sick, he couldn't carry all his luggage by him-self: he had a heavy sack and another rather voluminous parcel. "So what, do you want me to carry your luggage?" Vasile Ciolpan replied and slapped his face twice. Loaded as he was, with all his luggage, our friend took a few steps and then he collapsed. Only then, did the director give the order to the warden to take the luggage and it was brought to the prison on a bicycle. Another time, during a search, he found a cross that Sever Dan wore made of two pieces of wood. "What is this, punk?" the director yelled in anger and then he hit him over the head with it; after that he broke the cross in pieces and threw it on the floor. "If you want to pray, do it in your mind, don't use such things". He also hit others; many testimonies will, for certain, come up later. He also had violent verbal outbursts on occasions. At the time I was alone in cell twenty-one I heard him yelling at a section head once in connection with a prisoner: "Hit him over the head!"

In contrast to these gestures and words, he sometimes showed behavior which threw light on other aspects of his character. In July of 1950, in a moment of my deep depression, he told me: "Don't be so sad, you won't have to be here long." this phrase turned out to have no grounds: I stayed in prison for five more years *after that*; nevertheless it is true that he had had the intention to give me some hope. Also, he told Victor Papacostea, when he was in the boiler room, in the summer of the same year: "Relax, this will be over soon." It wasn't over soon, but his words were for Papacostea, as they were for me, a comfort which helped us to bear the months that followed. The most important request of those who were alone in their cells was to be moved into a group or, at least, to be given a cell-mate. While I was in cell number ten, in December of 1950, I put forward again, repeatedly and persistently, this request; the directors' response, always the same, was: "I don't decide the rearrangement of the prisoners; I get my orders from Bucharest." However, to show me that he wasn't personally against my request, he came to my cell one day, together with two section heads, and told me: "I brought you a cell-mate." I looked at him to see if he was joking and, at that moment, he held out his hand which he'd had behind his back: he had a sparrow in his hand. "Keep it in your cell and feed it bread crumbs; you will see, it will become tame; it will keep you company." I thanked him, and after they left, I set the sparrow free in the cell. The poor bird was in a terrible state of fear: beating itself against the walls and the windows; it seemed to have lost its' sense of direction. I put some crumbs on the cover of the tub and on the edge of the window; it didn't even look at them, and continued to fly in all directions and hurt itself. I felt pity for it and opened the window. After some more disordered flight in the room, it flew out the window and landed on one of the plum trees in the small yard; the other sparrows outside immediately began to chirp. A few hours later, at evening roll call, the director entered my cell again. "Where's the sparrow?" he asked immediately. "I set it free" I replied "it is enough to have one tormented soul in this cell; however, I thank you again for your gesture." "You made a mistake", he answered, "It would have helped you to pass the time."

Although a committed communist, when he had the impression that things could change, he didn't hesitate to try and smooth things over with the opposing side or at least – as Titu Maiorescu used to say – to establish a point of contact with the enemy. Thus, in October of 1950, when negotiations were ongoing at the United Nations concerning international control and a mission from the UN was supposed to come to Romania, he told me one afternoon when I complained again about the total isolation I was in: "Be patient, good things are coming for you." When I asked for explanations he didn't want to give me any; he just added: "It will be all right". I immediately put his words into the context of what I had learned during the past few days, through the window, from friends who told me about the negotiations in Geneva and I understood that this was a way for him to give me some good news in order to enhance my capability for resistance to prison. Another time, while I was in inmate group seventeen, and we informed him of a series of brutalities and obscene words from some of the section heads, he replied: "Well, if I weren't here it would be worse for you." In other words, what he wanted to say was that he was the one who restrained his subordinates, who would otherwise indulge in even tougher behavior.

***

About two or three times a year, the director was called to Bucharest. After such a trip, in the summer of 1950, he returned from Bucharest wearing a policeman's' uniform with the rank of Lieutenant. He held this rank until the beginning of 1954 when he was promoted to Lieutenant-Major. In November of 1953 a new secret police officer came to Sighet. He held the rank of Lieutenant-Major: three stars on his lapel. (Because of that, Niculae Sibiceanu quickly nicknamed him "Martel", after the brandy!). It was curious that the prison director had a lower rank; we guessed that he would be promoted soon, and that's what happened three months later. Vasile Ciolpan worked as the director of Sighet penitentiary until the spring of 1955; at the end of May he left.

The new director

He came in June of 1955, was fat and dark skinned, probably a gypsy. He held the rank of Lieutenant. Having worked as a warrant officer at the prison of the Ministry of the Interior, he was immediately recognized by Aurelian Bentoiu who had been imprisoned there in the autumn of 1944; he also met him in the prison on Bonaparte Road where he stayed from November 18, 1953 to the summer of 1954; by then, the warrant officer had become a Lieutenant.

The new director immediately established a series of regulations issued by the Ministry of the Interior that were not applied before in Sighet (or rather they were not applied very strictly). For example, continuous supervision through the observation holes. Day and night, *every two minutes*, sometimes even more often, the observation hole was opened and the section head peered into the cell. It bothered us, but it bothered the section heads more because they had to continually walk, for twelve hours, from one cell to another.

He also ordered that the mess tins be taken away from us as soon as we had finished eating; they were returned to us before the next meal; because of this measure it became impossible for us to have our own tin and to eat from the same tin each time; we received a different tin for every meal and many of us didn't like this. Some of the prisoners had the strange habit of washing their underwear and rags in their tins. As long as everyone kept their own tin, the results of this procedure were their own business; now, when the tins were circulating from one prisoner to the other, everyone risked the consequences of these procedures. This problem wouldn't have much importance from the point of view of hygiene because the tins were washed in the kitchen after each meal. (at least that's what we were told, and indeed most of the time we found them clean.) But in matters of food, the idea, the suggestion is very important and the thought that you could eat from a tin in which someone else had, a few hours earlier, washed his underwear ruins your appetite.

The third measure taken by the new director was the forbidding of speaking in a loud voice and of singing, even in a low voice. With this in mind, there was a very telling incident that took place in the middle of June of 1955. One late afternoon – in cell number seventeen – Aurelian Bentoiu, a music lover, was walking to the window where I was sitting, humming the aria "Salut, demeure chaste et pure" from the opera "Faust" by Gounod, softly. I listened to him with pleasure like always and when he was nearer to me, I told him with feeling: "That is a beautiful aria!" At that moment the door opened suddenly and the section head – a zealous Hungarian wanting to earn a promotion -asked: "Who sang?" There was a moment of silence, then he decided: "You two sang" and he pointed to us. We immediately protested, saying that we didn't sing; he replied: "Oh yes, you did sing; we'll see about that" and then he closed the door. After a few minutes, at evening roll call, the sub-Lieutenant who was on duty (we used to call him "Bibi") asked emphatically: "Who sang? Let him raise his hand himself". After a second, Bentoiu raised his hand, but he explained: "I didn't sing, I just hummed softly a tune for these suffering fellows." "What suffering fellows?" Bibi spat, and turning to the section head he ordered: "Bring the handcuffs immediately!" On his way out, the section head told Bibi from the door: "There was another one who sang too" and he pointed to me. I quickly protested energetically and Nicu Sibiceanu, the inmate group leader, confirmed that I didn't sing. He then left me alone; meanwhile the handcuffs arrived and they started to cuff Bentoiu. He protested indignantly against this procedure – not even in the high terror days, at the beginning of our detention, or in the time of "Gore" had such a punishment been applied – and, fully exasperated he said: "Why don't you shoot us instead of torturing us so much?" When they took Bentoiu out of the cell, the section head repeated for the third time: "There was another one who sang too" pointing at me again, but the sub-Lieutenant ignored his persistence. We believed that at nine in the evening, when the bell rings for "lights out" – in fact we slept with the lights on – Bentoiu would return. At nine o'clock our friend didn't show up. At around ten, the cell door was unlocked and the new director came in with a black look. He began an inquiry in order to discover who sang and what was sung. The majority of those in the cell told him – and this was the truth – that they didn't even hear anyone sing, so they didn't know what was sung. As for me, I repeated that I didn't sing and that Bentoiu only hummed – he didn't sing – and so softly that the majority of the others didn't even hear him. As for the tune that he had hummed, it was an opera aria. Following my words, the director started a furious speech, demanding that we tell him the truth: he said we were cultured people, people who had high positions; why don't we want to confess what we did and what we had sung? We looked at each other, puzzled, without understanding what he was getting at, when suddenly, turning to me he said accusingly: "It's useless for you to deny this; Bentoiu has already confessed, just here near the door when they took him upstairs: you both sang 'Long live the King'" I look at him and realize that this is a classic trick: they tell one person that his fellow already confessed and therefore he may as well not deny it. Then the same procedure is repeated with the other person; if one of the two is weak enough he falls in the trap and confesses. But this time I didn't have anything to confess: in reality I did not sing; as for the anthem that they say we sang, there's no question of singing it, although we both had it in our heart. Thus, it was easy for me to strongly deny this. I remember what I told him at a certain point: "You took everything away from us: freedom, fortune, and job; you swept away our families and there is only one thing we still have: our honor. I affirm on my honor, Mr. director, that I did not sing and that Bentoiu only hummed an opera aria and not 'Long live the King'". When I saw that he still looked at me with doubt, I added: "And if this is not enough for you, there is nothing left for me to do but to swear on my three children..." at that moment, he interrupted me, saying: "It is not necessary; but you must know that I will make you face Bentoiu tomorrow morning, because he confessed." "It is impossible that Aurelian Bentoiu confessed such a thing" I replied "And I demand to face him now, not tomorrow". "I am the one who decides when" he concluded and left the cell. Of course, there was no question of any confrontation the following morning; Bentoiu returned at about half past seven. He told us how they kept him handcuffed in "Neagra" for around three hours and then he was taken to the directors' office. The director ordered the handcuffs removed and started the interrogation, applying the same methods that he had used with me. He told him the same thing, and that it was useless to deny it because I had confessed. "It is impossible that Professor Giurescu admitted facts that didn't happen" replied Bentoiu quickly, requesting, as I did, to face me immediately. On this occasion, I found out that during the interrogation, the director characterized me, in front of my friend, as being a "bandit". Bentoiu replied: "He's not a bandit, he's one of our great historians."

We waited with curiosity to see what the director was going to do now after he played this game and in fact, was defeated. He came in our cell two days later and very calmly, as if nothing had happened, started to fill out some forms about the 'effects' we had on us. Not a word, not even a hint about what happened two days earlier.

The Deputy-Director

Before the spring of 1955 we didn't have a deputy-director. By the end of March or the beginning of April a tall, solid man with a full face came to the prison. He resembled Dr. Ghițescu, Victor Papacostea's' brother-in-law; that's why we named him "Ghițescu". By appearance and behavior he seemed rather sympathetic, although, in our cell he began by making a remark that we didn't deserve. He had told us that since his first visit he had wanted the cells' floor to be cleaned. We wanted the same thing but, during the last few weeks we'd had so much work to do that we literally didn't have time to take care of our own cell. We were the universal team that did all the work, from peeling vegetables for the kitchen to sweeping, washing and scrubbing the floors in the whole prison, pumping water, carrying coal and vegetables for the kitchen and unloading supplies and wood. When we asked, twice, to be given rags and brushes in order to clean the cells' floor we were turned down by the section head with the argument that there were other more urgent things to be done.

However, given the Lieutenants' wish, we insisted on getting the necessary things to clean the floors and eventually we managed to do that. But in the evening when he came for the roll call, the Lieutenant didn't notice what we had done – we really did our best, especially Nicu Sibiceanu and Gheorghe Strat who worked very hard – and he said that the floor wasn't clean. Maybe it was his fixation – I noticed that almost everyone in the prison staff had such a fixation – maybe the light was insufficient, but it's certain that he made this remark; it's true, he said it without malice, but he said it. During the weeks to follow we didn't have any reason to complain about him; he behaved decently. About a month before I left the prison, in the beginning of June – the new director having just arrived – the deputy-director came to our cell one morning and showed us what the new regulations were: we were not allowed to talk loudly or to sing; we were not allowed to hold any kind of lectures or conferences; we had to talk softly and only one on one. When someone in the staff entered the cell we had to turn our backs to him (sic!) and keep our faces to the window; during the roll call we were supposed to take the same position; if someone had anything to report, he should raise his hand

and after receiving permission from the duty officer, he could say what he had to say. A new innovation was that we had to sleep with our heads *toward the window*, so that the section head could see our faces at any time during the night, by looking through the observation hole. Our hands had to be kept in sight on top of the blanket, not underneath; this must have been done in order to prevent a suicide attempt: to prevent, for example, the prisoner from slashing his wrists with a piece of glass during the night.

The Duty Officers

The two duty officers, both sub-Lieutenants, came in the summer of 1954. One evening, when the director came for the roll call, we saw two new unknown faces in the hall in front of the cells' door: they were the future duty officers. While Nicu Sibiceanu, the leader of our group, was giving his report, Nicu Cornăţeanu and Victor Papacostea had a look at the two newcomers; I would have done the same thing if I'd had my glasses; but without my glasses I couldn't distinguish their physiognomies. Noticing my colleagues curiosity and probably irritated by the fact that they didn't look at him, and on the other hand in order to impress the newcomers, to show them how discipline must be given, the director had a violent outburst, one of those outbursts that showed his true character. In a contrast to the usual way he received reports he yelled at them: "What are you looking at, punk?" Cornăţeanu and Papacostea didn't know which of them he was addressing; in fact, he was addressing both.

Beginning with the next day, the newcomers started their job; we had had "duty officers" before then, but this role was played by under officers, warrant officers or sergeants; there had been three of them, each working twelve hours; while they were working their shift they wore red cloth armbands, with an inscription "duty officer".

One of the two sub-Lieutenants, very young – I guess he was under twenty-five – was nicknamed "Bibi", because he resembled Bibi Botez. He was a brunette with beautiful eyes and his fingernails were slightly purple; I had the impression that he was a gypsy or that he had some gypsy blood. He was an expert in metal work; this point made me guess at his gypsy origins. But there was the possibility that I was wrong and he didn't have such origins. In the beginning, his behavior was acceptable; we all agreed that we preferred him to his colleague, until he handcuffed Bentoiu for a trivial thing; starting with that day he became hateful to us. The other sub-Lieutenant, older than the first, resembled Raoul Bossy, our plenipotentiary minister in Italy; that's why we called him "Bossy". He had something hypo-critical, Jesuit-like in his behavior. In fact, he was a bad man and he was always looking for trouble. The days when he was on duty were more difficult for us than the others; he used to spy, going on tiptoe to the door of the cell and opening the shutter silently.

Of the under officers that occupied, before the two sub-Lieutenants came, the position of "duty officer", I will mention, first of all, the directors' brother-in-law, the so called "mime". I found out about his kinship to the director from one of the wardens; but I don't know what kind of brothers-in-law they were, I don't know whether one of them married the others' sister or whether they were married to two sisters.

He was about thirty to thirty-five years old, and of medium height, thin, he spoke very little and compensated by making gestures and having a very expressive face. From here comes his nickname; and also his second nickname, "the Mimetic", used especially by Gen. Nae Marinescu. The "mime" didn't like to make decisions; he didn't have urge to run things. He wasn't a bad man; during our five years I never saw him cursing or beating someone. He only reacted once, to make a decision to punish, but only because the fact was brought to his notice by the sentinel; if he were to do things his way, he probably wouldn't have taken any measure at all. In fact, he wasn't very fond of the communist regime, neither was he excessively zealous, like others who imagined that they would be promoted faster by being cruel. Probably, that is why he wasn't promoted as fast as the others; many others were before him. Maybe he was also handicapped by the fact that he liked to drink.

In fact, I noticed that many of the prison staff, beginning with the director, then his brother-in-law and finishing with the ordinary wardens, liked to drink. Maybe it was also a way of sedating their conscience, their concerns, of not thinking of the fact that they would have to pay for all the felonies carried out with their participation or done by them alone.

Another under officer who worked as a duty officer was "Păsărilă"[28] (*bird catcher*). We called him this – the idea belonged to

---

[28] *Translators' note:* 'Păsărilă', a character in a Romanian folk tale, was very tall.

the same Nicu Sibiceanu – because he was very tall, the tallest in the staff. He started to work in the prison as a section head; I found out that he had also spent some time in a madhouse, not as a warden but as a patient. He had a long swarthy face and a strange look in his eyes; sometimes he yelled like a crazy man. Other than this, judging from his behavior, you were tempted to think of him as a child. For example, he liked to play "choo-choo": in the night, after lights out, but also sometimes during the day, he used to squat and two section heads each took him by a hand and dragged him along the big hall, on a metal sheet which would cover the heating pipes. While they were dragging him, "Păsărilă" imitated the sound of a train engine and the steam whistle. After that, he used to take a long metal pipe and blow into it, making more sounds. He also knew how to play the recorder; he didn't play complicated tunes, only fragments of simple songs. He felt sympathy for Nicu Sibiceanu whom he called different names, especially "Pantelimoane" and "Şobolane"[29]; then he would turn to one of the section heads, telling him with admiration: "This is a heck of a guy". In fact Nicu knew, with jokes and appropriate remarks, how to disarm the worst section heads and even make them smile. Nicu had an undaunted spirit; he also knew great number of anecdotes, jokes and witticisms. On the other hand, he was always the first to work – it's true that he was the youngest and the strongest – and this gained him respect from the staff, the staff appreciating manual labor most of all.

Once, at the end of 1953 or the beginning of 1954 – the food had become better by then – after he gave us pasta, Păsărilă asked Sibiceanu: "Do you want more?" "I would like it, but I don't have anything to put it in: only maybe in my cap", answered Sibiceanu jokingly. "Do you want it in your cap?" "I do!" "Then here you are", and he filled the cap with pasta. We had terrific fun; for a long time after that Păsărilă used to ask him: "Don't you want any more in your cap?" and then laugh hysterically. At other times, when Păsărilă was having fits, he cursed in the filthiest possible way. Also, he contributed to our removal from the kitchen duty we loved, by reporting to the director a series of discussions, for example: the discussion on political issues between Romulus Pop and Gen. Marinescu, which took place in the spring of 1953.

---

[29] 'Şobolane' is a rat

The third of the duty officers recruited from among the under officers was "Pantoponul"; a funny name, which was given to him because, in a way, he was a sort of mime[30], but calmer than the other one. He was younger than the "mime" and had a blond, baby face and he seemed to have a very good position in the party or in the police department, because he was promoted twice, in a very short time during the autumn of 1953. He was civil, even polite; I never heard him say a rude word to a prisoner. In January of 1955, while I was isolated in cell number sixty, I was called to the 'effects room', to make a complete inventory of my belongings; on the way back, being accompanied by "Pantoponul", I asked him what he believed about our detention, and how long he thought it would last and when would we be released. He answered: "Very soon, very soon; it won't be long." It is improbable that he had secret information; I guess it was just a nice phrase, like I had heard many times before; however, I preferred this to hostile silence or some offensive words (like "Shut up!" or "You will stay here until you die!" or "How can you go home? You don't have a home anymore!"). On June 1, 1955, Dorel Dumitrescu, very seriously ill, was taken out of our group on the pretext that he would be sent to the hospital. At the following roll call, the leader of the group announced that only nine people were present instead of ten; "Pantoponul", who was on duty, showed an expression of compassion, yet futility on his face.

I am giving these details in order to show that not all the wardens in Sighet were brutes and beasts, that among them were kind hearted people, some of whom were really friendly. They understood our sorrow and suffering and tried, within the very restrictive limits of their duty, to alleviate it. The *system*, especially during the first three years, was bestial; the people were, as usual, mixed: some of them were mean, others were kind, the majority were neutral, but all of them were terrorized by the possibility that one of their co-workers could report them and therefore, they looked around with fear before saying a word. The mistrust of everyone for each other, spying on each other, these were the basic principles in the relationship among the prison's staff. There was an atmosphere of terror not only for the prisoners, but also for the wardens. "Here in prison is the biggest

---

[30] *Translators' note:* this is a play on the word 'pantomima' which means 'mime'

infamy" warden Gavrilă Pop from Vișeul de Sus told me one evening in January 1951 when he brought firewood for me, "We all shiver, not only you, but we too."

When I arrived in Sighet, I found a dark skinned warrant officer – the "Major", who was the head warden. He helped the director to make the inventory of our civilian effects; when I went to the effects room and gave up my things and was given, in exchange, the prisons' effects, he was the one who took responsibility for my belongings, while the director wrote the receipt. He was a very calm man; he treated the prisoners well, but he didn't stay long, maybe because of that; after a few months I didn't see him any longer.

The Wardens

Over the five years and two months we had a total of around forty wardens in Sighet; none of them stayed from the beginning to the end of the period I was in prison. Big changes in the warden staff took place in the autumn of 1953, in November, and in the autumn of 1954, beginning in September. Some of them stayed a very short time: they probably were not appropriate, because of their temper and behavior, for such a job.

The hatred for prisoners was systematically fed by regular meetings on Saturday and Wednesday. Meetings in which all kind of lies and slander were produced. Also, in these meetings the wardens were given slogans and expressions that I heard almost identically reproduced by some of them. It was a systematic action of continual embittering of the staff; in these meetings we were presented as "vampires" who "sucked the people's blood", "bestial landowners", "exploiters of the proletariat", bad guys who used to have "parties and orgies with champagne" and other things of this nature. I repeatedly heard all the above quoted words and expressions from the wardens; there were weeks when we heard the same slogans repeated many times. We laughed a lot in cell seventeen when the actor Ștefănescu-Goangă was called a "Vampire" who sucked the peoples' blood" by one of the "indoctrinated" wardens. It was a very funny connection between the two words "Goangă"[31] and "Vampire", and we laughed a long time over that.

The wardens also had imprinted in their minds contempt for what

---

[31] 'Goangă' means insect

was the leading class in the past; this class was the symbol of sin, incompetence and dishonesty, in contrast, of course with the present leading class (the communist class), which concentrates all virtues and knowledge within it.

Each one of these wardens had, like any other man, people whom he sympathized with and people whom he disliked among the prisoners. Thanks to this fact, we were able to establish contacts, to receive information and, during the starvation period, to get extra food.

Sibiceanu managed to become the most liked by the wardens; from some of them, for example "the Aviator", he got very precious information, about international events as well as about what happened inside the country and in the prison.

I was particularly liked by "Cireşică"[32] and "the Aviator". The true name of the former was *Ştefan Paşcu* and he was from Ţigăneştii-Criş (Bihor County). He gave me this information one day in the winter of 1951-52, when I was isolated in cell twenty-one. He asked me, on this occasion, whether I was a "father"; for him, a devout Uniate, being a priest meant the highest social position; when I told him that I was a Professor at the University, I could see the disappointment on his face. It is very likely that he was connected to the Uniate priests in prison and used to give them information. *Gavrilă Pop*, from Vişeul de Sus, also liked me; he told me his name and where he was from, and this was a sign that he trusted me a lot, because the wardens were strictly forbidden to tell the prisoners about their true identity. He used to bring me, now and then, stealthily, raw carrots from the cellar; this was in the period of chronic hunger; such a gift was very precious also because it contained vitamins, and we almost didn't get vitamins at all.

Despite my efforts, I could only find out the names of a small number of the wardens. Besides the two above mentioned wardens, there was *Pintea*, one of the wardens that we found there when we arrived at Sighet, who also told me his name. His father was a well-off peasant in Transylvania; he had a few years of high school and he didn't like being a warden in the prison. He told me that he wanted to leave, to return home and find another job; this job, he didn't like.

I also found out other names, not from them directly, but thanks to the fact that they were called by name by their co-workers. Thus, I

---

[32] 'Cireşică' is a small cherry

discovered the name of *Boca* – a short wall-eyed man, of *Arba* – the man with snake eyes, of *Ionescu* – a sort of Bucharest tramp and of *Veress* a Romanian with a Hungarian name. We gave *conventional names* to all the others in order to be able to identify them when we talked among ourselves. We were inspired either by their resemblance to known persons or by their previous profession which we found out by gossip, or by specific body features, their speech or their temperament. Finally, some of them were identified by initials and numbers, the initials being the first letter of the words expressing the moral category which we, in our opinion, put them in. Thus, there were a series of B's (for "Beast"), namely B-1, B-2, B-3 and B-4; then a series of C's (for "Cur"), namely C-1, and C-2.

I will describe, in the following pages, the wardens, with their real or conventional names; I will also give some details about each of them, based upon things that I know or upon things that my fellows told to me.

Pintea was one of the best wardens that we had. Kind hearted, ready to joke, he had a real sympathy for the prisoners. He asked us immediately who we were, where we were born, where we lived and what jobs we had had before. When he came with a tub of beans, he used to ask me whether I wanted "thin or thick", i.e. with more soup or with more beans. He asked that because some of us – later I was in this situation – could not tolerate the beans. When we received a watery soup of "Călărabe" or "Breasbe" i.e. turnip or cabbage, he used to say, mocking the prison: "Even in Paris they don't have soup like this" and he would grimace with disgust. At other times he used to call this soup "tea" and to invite us: "Would you care for some tea?". In the morning, when he came with the dish of warm water smelling of lime, he used to say ironically: "Come and get coff-feh" i.e. coffee (pronounced in a German accent). The fellows in inmate group seventeen told me that in the evening, between the roll call and lights out, he sometimes came to give them cigarettes and talk to them. In the autumn of 1950 when he returned from a one month holiday, when he saw the fellows in cell seventeen he told them with sincerity: "I hoped not to find you here anymore". Pintea also liked to drink now and then. In the first year, in October, I saw him "plastered" once. He opened my cell door and weaving back and forth, he brought his hand to his cap and, with slurred speech he told me: "I have the honor. How are you?" He probably had "tasted" too much wine. Starting with the beginning of 1951, I didn't see Pintea anymore.

In contrast to Pintea, B-1 was bestial. He had a mongoloid face – that's why we called him the "Mongoloid" – he had prominent cheekbones and a dirty pustulant complexion. There were, obviously, months when he did not bathe and when he came close to us, he smelled so bad that we felt like we wanted to puke. He shaved me twice, cutting up my face; the bad odor was so awful that I almost didn't feel the pain. He yelled and cursed all the time, "Damn", "Christ" and "Sons of bitches" were the favorites in his speech. When he came with the food or opened the door in order to take us for the "walk" or to the toilet, he always added: "Move faster!" in a very insulting tone. From all he said and did, one could see a deep hatred for us. I have rarely seen a more cruel and hate-filled man.

Arba belonged to the same category. He walked bowleggedly -he had bowed legs like cowboys do – his eyes were like those of a snake, with a metallic cold glare. He couldn't pronounce the word "two"; when he called the section head on the second floor he always said "Too-wah", so that it was sufficient enough to only hear the word to know from the pronunciation that the speaker was Arba. I found out from the fellows that, in our heyday, he had been sentenced to many years of forced labor – about five, it seems – for murder; he had killed a policeman. The communists released him from the prison and made him a warden: it's obvious that this is why he was so devoted to them. He also cursed like B-1 and took sadistic pleasure in tormenting and humiliating the prisoners. For example, he made us wash the floor of the hall and corridors three times with the complaint that it wasn't done properly. In the spring of 1951, I suffered from jaundice, a rather serious form of jaundice: it lasted for three months. One morning at my sickest, and yellow all over my body as if I was painted with saffron, I was taken out in the big yard and allowed to sit on a tree stump in the sun, with the warden watching me. Arba came, sat down on a stack of wood and, looking at me, said: "You know you can die of this disease?" It is easily imaginable how much pleasure this remark gave me. I contented myself to answer: "Thank you for your encouragement". The warden who watched me looked persistently at Arba, who probably felt embarrassed and added: "I didn't say it on purpose to you, but you know" – and he repeated – "you can die of it". After that, he stood up and left. You must have a very unkind heart to tell someone such a thing when they are ill! Even the warden was disgusted; he pushed his cap back and said under his breath: "He's a mother-fucking bastard". The same Arba, in June of 1950, opened the cell door one day at the exact moment I was stepping down from the bed; I had gotten up on the bed in order to look out the window because there was a group of prisoners in the yard and I wanted to know who they were. Because I had heard noise in the hall I stepped down immediately. Arba wasn't sure whether I'd looked out the window, therefore he began by asking me: "Did you look out of the window?" I denied it, because I'd only intended to look but hadn't because of his entrance. Also, I knew from those who were in prison earlier that if you confess that you committed something or intended to commit something then the punishment is unavoidable. "I'm taking you to 'Neagra'!" he told me and we went to that cell which was on the second floor. While we were ascending the stairs, he asked me again; I denied it. When we arrived in front of "Neagra" he asked me the same question for the third time, but he added: "If you confess, I won't punish you; If you don't confess you will stay naked in 'Neagra' until tomorrow morning." We were in the first period, of out-breaks of hatred and aggression, when the penalties were coming one on top of another, when the "Neagra" was functioning all the time. Seeing that I didn't say anything, he insisted: "Confess and nothing bad will happen to you; I promise you". I had the weakness – not to mention the naiveté – to believe him; I hadn't had a situation like this with him before; so I confessed that I had had the intention to look out of the window and that, because of that I had climbed on the bed; but I had heard a noise in the hall and I had gotten down. "So you confess that you wanted to look out of the window; go into 'Neagra'". Thus, I entered naked into that awful cell, realizing that the Frenchmen are right when they recommend, in court; "N'avouez jamais!" (Never Confess). After two hours, the duty officer – the dark skinned warrant officer, the "Major" as Pintea used to call him -came and let me out of "Neagra". While I dressed, he asked me why I was punished. I told him the entire story; when I finished, he spat between his teeth and told me in a comforting tone: "Damn that son of a bitch!" A week later, Arba wanted to provoke me to look out the window. There was a group of prisoners chopping wood in the big yard, I noticed that in the morning: it was Cornăţeanu's group. Suddenly, I saw a hand making signs outside in front of the window. This was so unusual – the sentinel in the watchtower supervised any movement of those in the yard – that I didn't have to be too smart to see that it was an act of trickery, and a very stupid one. Of course, I didn't react to this, and was even amused at seeing the methods he used. He repeated the gesture three or four times, with the same result. Irritated by the fact that I didn't react, he eventually gave up saying to one of his colleagues: "The son of a bitch doesn't want to look out". After hearing his voice, I realized that it was Arba. Since that time, knowing that he was after me, I was very careful whenever he was on duty. I have to add that this same man, in August, while I walked in the small yard where tomatoes and potatoes were growing, came to me and urged me to take two tomatoes; the tomatoes were just starting to ripen and for us, who hadn't seen fruits or vegetables for three months, tomatoes were priceless. I had asked repeatedly at the roll call – Arba being present – for vegetables and fruit but received the standard answer: "It is not possible: this is not on your ordered menu". I insisted, invoking our lack of vitamins, so that all the section heads knew me as being "the vitamin man". Thus, my natural reaction would have been to take the tomatoes immediately; I hesitated however, out of fear that this could be a new trap; I knew him very well. Seeing that I didn't move, he urged me again and, eventually, he picked two tomatoes and handed them to me. Maybe he was sorry for what he had done to me before, or maybe he wanted to have a better relationship with me (since the incident with "Neagra" I had the habit of looking into his eyes whenever I met him, without saying a word) I cannot say precisely. However, I tend to believe that the second explanation is the right one. I noticed many times that the wardens didn't like the prisoners to stare at them, especially when combined with silence. "Why are you staring at me?" they used to say in these situations. "Don't look at me like that!". They had the impression that they saw, in our eyes, not only a reproach but a threat.

***

Boca was of short to medium height and he was wall-eyed. Extremely conceited, he had an excellent opinion of himself and his abilities. For example, he believed that he knew how to mend different utilities. In reality, he actually ruined what he tried to mend. A tap which was "repaired" by Boca didn't work anymore or would work very badly. He used to carry a hammer with him and hit the thing he wanted to repair until he ruined it completely. But because of his vanity, sometimes you could make him do things for you – especially give you extra food – if you resorted to exploiting this feature of his character. He gave great importance to the authority he had, or rather that he believed he had. Anyway, he liked to give orders and behave importantly. One day, at the end of May or the beginning of June of 1950, Dinu Brătianu had been taken outside to the big yard; being sick and unable to walk, he was given a chair; the chair was just in the line of sight of my window, close to the angle between the main body and the right wing of the building. Being on duty that day, Boca came over to him and asked him: "Do you know me?" "No, I don't know you" answered Dinu. "Try to remember, when you used to hunt around Bucharest." "No, I still don't remember you." Dinu repeated. "I was a small boy, one of the beaters" Boca continued, "And I remember you from then". Seeing that he got no response, he changed the question: "Well, why don't you go hunting now? Maybe you can't?" "I am imprisoned now and have no rifle" the old man answered, hoping that he would be left alone. "I think you have hunted enough, let other people hunt now" Boca concluded. I heard this conversation very clearly; I believe the wardens claim that he was one of the beaters in Ciornuleasa or Tîncăbești where Dinu usually went hunting, is pure invention, a lie. In reality, Boca, who has a Transilvanian accent, only wanted to stress his importance and irritate the old man.

I had problems with this man two months after I arrived in Sighet. We had just been given feces containers and we were sup-posed to empty them every morning, in the toilet. This operation used to be done one at a time, beginning with the cell near the exit and ending with the cell at the end of the big hall. My cell, number twenty-one, was second to last. When I went with the container to the toilet, I saw a puddle on the cement floor around the toilet opening. This opening was made by my predecessors, some of them elderly or maybe ill, not having the strength to lift the container and empty it so that the liquid doesn't splash out of the hole. Boca appeared near the door when I rinsed my container with clean water and began to yell: "You made a puddle on the floor; I will make you lick it up." I looked at him and

said calmly: "I didn't spill a drop." "Yes you did, I saw you." "You
didn't see anything" I replied, "because at the moment you appeared
in the door I had finished and was rinsing the container." "Clean the
floor immediately; I want to see the moon and the bulb shine on the
floor otherwise you're in trouble." he continued, not caring who did it.
"I want to see the moon and the bulb" was the favorite expression of
the wardens; they probably had the impression that the "moon", as in
the old expression, wasn't sufficient and they added the contemporary
"bulb" (electric bulb), making it a new symbol of cleanliness and, of
the two joint terms, the superlative. "I have nothing to clean with." I
answered, and I really didn't have anything. "with your cap!" he
yelled. "I won't do it with my cap because I would ruin it and not be
able to wear it anymore." "Are you cleaning or not?" he yelled again
and advanced two steps. "I didn't make the puddle; however in order
to not be accused that I disobeyed an order, I will clean it if I'm given
a broom." the refusal to carry out an order was considered the same as
a serious offense and – I was warned – that it was harshly punished.
They had in their minds the idea that you disobeyed them in order to
stand up to them, to express your contempt for them in this way, and
this drove them out of their minds, transforming them into beasts.
"There is no broom" – actually there were three brooms on the first
floor – and he gave me a hand-sized rag: "So, then do it with this". I
had to clean up, soaking the rag in urine and wringing it out in the
hole. This procedure took around five minutes; it was not only
disgusting but also unhygienic. When I had finished, he came close to
me, he looked at the floor and said: "It's not good; wipe the liquid
again". I had taken all of the liquid, but the beast, irritated because I
had contradicted him and I hadn't carried out his order immediately
and I had argued about it, had decided to break me. "There's nothing
left", I replied, "I wiped up all the liquid." "Shut up and wipe;
otherwise I will make you scrub it until evening." "I will report this
mockery to the director." "You can report; which one of us do you
think he'll believe? It's still me whom he'll believe; scrub and don't
say a word, you son of a bitch." "I will report you for cursing too." I
continued and, at the same time, I began to scrub again. I scrubbed
for another five minutes, without making a difference, just because he
wanted this; after that the beast snapped at me from the door: "Get
your ass to your cell." I took the container and without having the
chance to wash my hands ("you will wash your hands in your cell") I

returned to my cell. In the evening, I reported this to the section head when the shift changed – this was Pintea – and I added that I also wanted to report this to the director. "I will tell the director" he answered and closed the door. A half an hour later Pintea appeared again – this time he was alone – and stepping into the cell he told me in a low voice: "This Boca is a son of a bitch; this is how he is; don't give too much importance to this. And you should know that the director" he continued "won't stick up for you; he is also afraid that someone will tell on him; here it's dog eat dog". I thanked him and I realized that he was right. No matter what you reported, the director would never be, at least in public, on your side. The next experience taught me that if a warden was kind, if he treated the prisoners well, he didn't stay long at Sighet. With the exception of those who knew how to *simulate*, to give the *impression* of being tough, saying bad words *only when the other staff was present* and then, when alone being well behaved and even helpful; all the others didn't stay long. Simulation is another feature of the system: people say things that they don't believe, they express opinions and feelings that they don't have and that in their soul they contest and even despise.

The "Habsburg" was called this because he had a Germanic look, with blond hair and fine features. He was a Hungarian or maybe half Hungarian and half German. He spoke very good Hungarian and very bad Romanian, with an accent which immediately showed his origins. Being scoliotic he had a distinctive way of walking; when he walked down the hall, I recognized him by his paces, even if he didn't say anything. He had a quick temper; he liked us to do the work fast, even very fast, without taking into account the prisoners' effort, his age or his health. When he saw that things were not done as fast as he wanted, he became angry; he began to tremble with rage and yell, and sometimes to hit and curse; he had real hysteria. Like Boca, he was also extremely conceited; he thought he was the center of the universe; everything had to revolve around him. "When I give an order, not even Christ can change it"; he considered himself more important than the duty officer or the director. He loved that his section always finished any job first: the feces containers, the cleaning, the distribution of food. When we carried the tubs of food, at noon and in the evening, he used to tell us confidentially: "Bring it to me first", in this way coming in conflict with his own co-workers at times. He was on good terms with Sibiceanu and, for a long time, on bad terms with Papacostea.

Once, while we were carrying things to the cellar, he pushed Papacostea down the stairs and cursed at him; when Papacostea, who was sick, protested and said that Habsburg could have killed him, Habsburg replied: "So what if you die? There will be one bandit less". He used to call us names whenever he got mad and, unfortunately, he got mad often and easily, without any apparent reason. He overdid things in order to be promoted faster; that's why he was very surprised when others were promoted and he remained "good at his rank". Eventually he was promoted together with all of the others. He liked to torment people, to make them do senseless work.

One day, while I was on the kitchen team, he made us wash the floor of the corridor; as soon as we had finished it, he remembered that the walls and the ceiling of the corridor had to be dusted with brushes; we did this; obviously, the dust fell on the floor, so we had to wash it again. When we were done, he made us clean the heating system pipes and the doors in the corridor; we cleaned them; but as we working in the hall the floor became dirty again, because of our wet boots. The result was that we washed the floor for the third time.

Sometimes it dawned upon him that there were too many people on the cleaning team and then he would decide that the work that was usually done by six people could be done only by one or two. He didn't accept any suggestions: he had the impression that accepting advice or suggestions from one of the prisoners would be a "Capitio diminutio"; he always said that he knew best. I suffered the greatest humiliation – not even now can I forgive myself for it – together with all of the fellows in group thirteen, when the "Habsburg" forced us to stay kneeling in the cell. It was one afternoon in the summer of 1954, immediately after lunch. We had just finished lunch and he was busy taking the prisoners to the toilet on the third floor. We were talking among ourselves, no louder than usual, in our cell on the first floor. It so happened that I and my neighbor didn't speak. The sentinel probably wanted to show off. In order to show how "vigilant" he was, he called the section head. When "Habsburg", on the third floor, asked why he was called ("What's the matter?") the sentinel answered that on the first floor the prisoners had spoken loudly, and pointed to our cell. Angry that he was disturbed in his work and had to descend to the second floor and then again to the first, he charged enraged to our cell and began to scream: "Why do you speak so loudly?" The group leader told him that nobody had talked louder than usual, and this made him even more angry: "The sentinel told me!" – he yelled – "You talked loudly. As punishment, you will all kneel on the floor." We protested strongly against this punishment, saying that we didn't deserve it and that it was humiliating. He didn't want to hear anything; he was enraged; he threatened with an ugly face, eyes popping out of his head: "If I don't find you kneeling in three minutes, when I return, you'll see what will happen to you!" and he left, slamming the door. We talked to see what we could do; Sibiceanu and I had the opinion that we must obey; Gen. Nae Marinescu said that it would be better to humor the crazy man and he was the first to kneel, with the others following him. I remembered that, on another occasion, Miluță Romașcanu was forced to kneel by this same man; I believed at that time that it was his idea, although Habsburg said that one of his superiors had given the order, not him. I didn't believe him but later, I found out that the director had given him the order to force prisoners to kneel. I looked at the other prisoners: they were all kneeling; Sibiceanu and I knelt too. In about ten minutes, the beast returned, he canceled this punishment and began to talk to us as if nothing had happened. "That's the way you are, you speak loudly" and then told us that he was upset because he had had to come down from the third floor and we had interrupted his work. While he was speaking to us, not too loud, the sentinel called him again. "What do you want?" Habsburg asked, going out into the yard. "They are talking loudly again" and he pointed again to our cell. "What the hell...? I was there" and he returned to our cell. It was easy for us, by this very fact, to show him that the same thing had happened the first time and so we were innocent. But we had already been punished. We reported after that to the security officer, "Martel". But I think "Habsburg" wasn't punished for this, or at least we didn't hear about any measures taken against him. He worked on duty for a while "at the entrance", without being in direct contact with the prisoners, but at the end of January he returned to his duty in the sections. Actually, the "entrance" was part of the regular job, each warden working there in turn.

This same man, after he calmed down and especially when he had the feeling that he went overboard or he was unjust, was given to gestures of kindness. He came to us many times with extra food; for example, one day he brought us a half a bucket of a meat dish, almost completely meat; we then had food supplies for two days; Sibiceanu

and Cornățeanu, who were, beyond any doubt, the biggest eaters, put
aside an impressive supply. Miluță Romașcanu, being too full and not
setting anything aside, regretted this later.

I found out about "Habsburg" – from him – that he was married
and had two children and before this he had worked as a waiter in a
restaurant. He also used to talk about the maid that he hired for his
wife, but probably, being conceited and a braggart, this was pure
invention; it seemed that the salary of a warden with a family was not
big enough for him to hire a maid. While we were working in the
kitchen, one day two prisoners in our group met two priests in the
corridor who were working in the bathroom. Such encounters,
breaking the "secret", were very unpleasant for the wardens on duty,
being one of the biggest failures for them. "Habsburg" was on duty
that day. When he saw this catastrophe – it was his fault that he didn't
do something, ensuring that the priests didn't leave the bathroom – he
yelled at my fellows to put their heads down – in order to not see "the
boys" – and for them to immediately return to the kitchen. Dumitru
Nistor – one of the two fellows – who, on principle, didn't want to
obey wardens orders immediately – especially as he got very bored
when he was told to "move faster" – did not hurry and didn't put his
head down. "Habsburg", seeing him, rushed to him and threw him
into the kitchen, saying "Look at him, he keeps his head up like a
painted whore!" We laughed for a long time about this outburst; for a
long time we called Nistor "Marshall Cur-wei-wop". Why
"Marshall"? This, as Kipling says, is another story.

"Pithecanthropus erectus" was one of the most bestial wardens that
we had in Sighet if not the most bestial. A serious alcoholic, with the
face of a degenerate, growling rather than speaking. When you saw
him for the first time you had the impression that he was a "minus –
habens", hence his nickname, which was given not only by group
number seventeen but also by another group. He used to drink so
much, and he was so intoxicated with alcohol that he fell asleep in
unusual places. I found him once, sleeping wrapped in his coat, on
the big rocky stairs; he had his head on one of the steps and his feet
five steps below. When he spoke, in a drawling nasal voice, as if he
was half asleep, one could say that the man was not stupid and
sometimes he even had a sense of humor. We found out from him
that he was sent, during the Antonescu government, to Germany to
work in a factory. He stayed in Hamburg and assisted in several

bombardments; "When I saw them coming, I hid under a willow tree near a bunker. I suddenly heard: Boom – fuck it, everything was pulverized – " He was married and had two children; "The small one is damn smart, he resembles me".

He was greedy, he stole from the meager food of the prisoners. He used to shamelessly cut pieces of our helpings of bread and marmalade with his penknife; sometimes he took the marmalade completely. We saw him, my colleagues and I, doing this many times. One day, he came to the kitchen and told Sibiceanu "Nicu, I have to tell you something: there is not enough marmalade." "Were you short a helping, Sir?" asked Nicu, wanting to be polite, because he was certain all the helpings were there; but knew that "Pithecanthropus" had helped himself to some helpings. "Not one helping, but seven; you understand?" he replied. "It's not possible, Sir, they were all there", answered Sibiceanu. "Oh yes, all?" and then "Pithecanthropus" left without persisting; that day some of the prisoners did not get their bits of marmalade: forty grams in two days, i.e. twenty grams a day (0.7 ounce).

In the beginning of March of 1952, one afternoon, I was near the kettle with my friend Cornățeanu; "Pithecanthropus" was on duty. He came to us in order to light a cigarette and while we were chatting he told us that he wasn't a bad man, that he didn't use to punish the prisoners. We hadn't gotten to know him yet, we didn't know what he was capable of; we had been working for only a short time in the kitchen, and he had only been in Sighet for a short time. Several days later, Cornățeanu, again working in the kitchen, preparing the food, tasted a piece of gristle to see whether it was good. Just then "Pithecanthropus" entered the kitchen; "You're eating meat, aren't you?" he said and, without waiting for an answer he added: "Let's go to 'Neagra'!" Cornățeanu explained to him, but in vain, that it was his duty to taste the food and see if it was done; but the beast didn't want to listen to him. Probably he was also drunk. "So, there you were eating meat" he said again when they arrived near "Neagra" and, suddenly, he slapped Cornățeanu. The slap was so hard that we heard it in the kitchen. Then we heard Cornățeanu screaming for help. My friends reaction (normal!) impressed "Pithecanthropus"; he stopped slapping him and after he locked him in the cell, he came downstairs.

On the afternoon of April 24, 1953, we were in our cell, number seventeen, when at half past four or five we heard the voice of

Gheorghe Brătianu in the yard. He had been taken out for the "walk" and, from what he was saying, we understood that he had an argument with a section head who was supervising him, the famous "Pithecanthropus". "What are you doing there?", we heard the latter saying, "Where did I tell you to go?" "You told me to come here" Gheorghe Brătianu answered. He seemed to be looking for a rag or a broom, to clean the yard with; we couldn't see what happened outside, we only heard it. "Here?" the beast replied and then we heard a fist hitting something. "Damn you son of a bitch; I'll show you!" the beast continued. And after a few seconds: "Move your ass upstairs". When they arrived, on the catwalk of the second floor we heard him hitting Brătianu again, this time he slapped him, then we heard the cell door opening violently and then a series of curses. This was the last straw; during the night – April 24-25, 1953 – Gheorghe Brătianu killed himself, by slashing his own throat.

"Luvaţi" had an oriental face, with slanted eyes and prominent cheekbones. He was solid, with a broad back, and well built; the job suited him; while other wardens lost weight, becoming skin and bones – for example the "mime" – he became fat. He wasn't a Romanian; maybe he was a Ukrainian, with some Tartar blood, maybe even a full Tartar. He spoke good Russian and bad Romanian. He couldn't pronounce the 'v' at the beginning of words; therefore he used to say "oi" instead of "voi" (meaning 'you'), "iu" instead of "viu" (meaning 'alive'), "ai" instead of "vai" (meaning 'alas'). When he became angry he threatened: "Iu la oi şi ai de oi" instead of "Viu la voi şi vai de voi" (I am coming to you and it will be bad for you). At other times, when he gave us food that we had to share among ourselves, he used to say "Daţi la oi" instead of "Daţi la voi" (The former means 'give it to the sheep' and the latter 'give it to each other'). He used to add a 'v' into the middle of the word between two vowels; thus, instead of "luaţi" (take) he would say "luvaţi". Therefore we nicknamed him "Luvaţi", and sometimes we also used to call him "Daţi la oi". He was a man of regulations; if one of his superiors told him to do something, he could be sure that "Luvaţi" would carry it out exactly. He was very respectful, obedient, even humble with his superiors. Even in front of the lower ranked Corporal, he was always ready to do everything in order to hear a good word or a favorable remark from him. "Come on, move faster, the Corporal ordered that", and he used to tell us, conveying one of the Corporals' orders; that he was ready to stand at attention and click his heels at any word from the Corporal. Very poor – maybe he had a large family – he was very stingy. He used to gather the cigarette butts from the hall, making unfair competition with the prisoners who didn't have any other possibilities to get something to smoke. He wasn't very good at reckoning; one day, when we weighed the potatoes in the cellar, we made the calculations for him and he said, very satisfied: "E bine la oi" (he had wanted to say 'you are good' but had said 'it's good to be with sheep'). He was mean when he had the feeling that someone didn't carry out his orders quickly enough or commented on them; he had the feeling – given his inferiority complex – that the delay or the comment were because the prisoner didn't take him seriously or mocked him; in these situations he became cruel.

One day, while we were in cell seventeen, laying on our beds, he came in and told us to go to the kitchen. Dumitru Nistor lingered a moment on the bed and when "Luvați" criticized him for laying on the bed Dumitru answered that we were allowed to do that. "So, you are talking back to me! O.K., you stay here!". We found out later, after we returned from work, that "Luvați" had made him, as punishment, stay for half an hour squatted on his haunches with his arms outstretched in front of him without being allowed to lean on the bed. This position, that we called the "bustard" became tiresome after a few minutes and, really painful after fifteen minutes. Nistor went through a big hardship that day; when we returned he was congested and he had a headache; suffering from arterial sclerosis, he had run a big risk. To make sure that Nistor served his penalty correctly and didn't lean on the bed, "Luvați" checked him through the observation opening every two or three minutes or he opened the door saying: "I will teach you not to talk back to me again". When I returned from isolation, in February of 1955, into group seventeen, the fellows told me that while I was absent "Luvați" used to check all the cells after lights out to see whether the prisoners slept. When he found someone with their eyes open he yelled through the observation opening: "Close you eyes when I order you to!" When he was interested in you he knew how to be polite or even nice.

At the time when they were raising two pigs in the prison, the sows' piglets were shared between the wardens with families - "Luvați" was one of these. Miluță Romașcanu had among other activities, the chore of feeding the pigs. This was convenient for him, because, carrying the bucket with leftover food or water, he had the opportunity to make many trips daily to the main hall and the kitchen corridor and gather the cigarette butts which were extremely valuable for an addicted smoker, which he was. Whenever he saw him carrying the bucket, "Luvați" was happy; of course he allowed him to circulate in the hall whenever he asked to; if any trouble came up concerning how the pigs should be fed, "Luvați" use to say, with a benevolent smile, turning to Miluță: "This is something he knows; he is 'the boss'"

"The Barber" wasn't in Sighet when I arrived there; he came a few months later; he was one of the very few who stayed there until July of 1955, being a man that the party trusted. Generally he had a satisfactory attitude towards us. He was tall with a thin face and a little bit wall-eyed originating from Transylvania, he had been a prisoner in Russia for a few years and had come back from there a communist. He told me that it was very hard at the beginning when he was a prisoner: he had to work in a mine, and the work was hard, exhausting; because of the insufficient food and fatigue he had weighed less than 110 pounds. Later, things were better. He knew how to shave and cut hair; therefore he was the prison barberfor more than three years; at the same time he was the gravedigger, at night, when the corpses had to be buried on the banks of Iza. He often had a sad, tormented air; it was as if something oppressed him; maybe it was the images of those who died in prison whom he'd had to bury.

When I was suffering from jaundice, in the spring of 1951, and I looked like skin and bones, he told me, in contrast to what Arba had said, words of encouragement; he told me about someone whom he knew with a serious form of jaundice and who got well by using traditional remedies; twice he poured rubbing alcohol on my head: "This is good for you" he said and added quickly: "Don't tell anybody that I gave you this".

When we, those from group eighteen, wanted to make a suggestion or wanted a certain measure to be taken, we first talked to him. We showed him what things were like, enumerated our points and often got a result. He never beat you or cursed; but sometimes, probably after a meeting where we'd been criticized, he used to make ironic hints to "the gentlemen ministers". Only once did I see him irritated, even furious: it was in the summer of 1953, in a time of strict discipline, when he made Miluță Romașcanu do "the frog" three hundred times.

By the end of 1953 or the beginning of 1954 he wasn't the barberanymore, being replaced by "Ciripică". Since that time we called him "the Ex". He started to work as a section head; when he replaced, because of a short absence, the new barber he told me that he could have gone to a school and become an officer. "But I didn't want this; it is better, in these times, to be smaller". Several days before I was released, on the first or second day of July, one of us complained that we were imprisoned for such a long time without any news from home. "The ex" said something that impressed me: "Don't worry, it's going to be all right". The way he said it, with warmth and a good smile, gave us the impression that it wasn't only something nice to say as we'd been told so many times before. In addition, a large inquiry commission had been working for three months in a room on the second floor. Our impression was correct: on July 5, some of us were told that we were going to leave Sighet and that we'd have mandatory domicile in Măzăreni (Brăila County), and that consequently we would be able to see our families. The others were told that they would be sent to Malmaison in Bucharest. After a short time they were also released.

"The Aviator" was tall, well built with a face that inspired sympathy from the beginning. He was probably from the old kingdom, from Muntenia, judging from his speech. Before joining the police, he had worked in aviation; he showed the fellows in group eighteen an old aviator card; he told them that he had, shortly after the war, the chance to join the American aviators; at that time he had hesitated; now he was sorry for not having done it. When he began with the police he didn't believe that he would become a warden; if he had known, he wouldn't have joined the police. It was very clear that he didn't like the profession of being a warden; in fact, he made that very clear to us one afternoon when we were in the yard chopping wood. That same day he gave us details about one of his adventures, during the Antonescu government, in 1941 or 1942. He wasn't an aviator at that time; he was doing his military service in the Buzău mountains, as a border guard, near the new border with Hungary. One day, when he was patrolling, he ran into a patrol of Hungarian soldiers who had gotten lost and had entered our territory. He ordered them to halt, arrested them and took them to the guard house. Following an agreement between the Romanians and Hungarians, the patrol was sent back; he himself accompanied them to a town in Transylvania where he handed them over to the Hungarian authorities. He couldn't stand the Hungarians and the Jews; he told us this, without embarrassment, that afternoon in the yard while we were chopping wood.

In the town of Sighet he met a widow with two children who was sort of well-off: she had a house in town and some land. He married her and one year later, they had a little boy. He was very proud of his son and used to tell us how healthy the boy was; when the boy became sick with an ear infection – his ear was leaking slightly – "the Aviator" asked Gen. and Doctor Nae Marinescu for advice and the General told him the necessary treatment; a few days later he told us, happily, that the boy had gotten well.

Of all the wardens in Sighet "the Aviator" was the most useful *to us*. He used to give us – through Sibiceanu – news and information; he told us what the newspapers and the radio were saying. During the Korean War, he kept us informed of what was happening; one day, after some terrible American bombardments, that the communist newspapers and radio had protested against, he told us that in Romania the communists were worried – 'were changing their shorts' in fear – that the same thing would happen here and create a war.

Whenever he could, he gave us extra food; he came once with a loaf of bread, his helping – the wardens used to be given bread, meat and other foods from the prison; for them and their families – and gave it to us to share among those of us who were working in the kitchen; another time he brought us cherries; he used to give cigarettes to the smokers or sometimes he just left a lit cigarette on the edge of the table or counter.

When I was alone in cell twenty-one, he brought me milk twice; there had been a little milk left over from those who were sick and got diet food, and he gave it to me; it didn't represent very much from the point of view of my food but the gesture, like all similar gestures, was very touching.

"The Aviator" warned us *to be careful with the informers*. Unfortunately in Sighet there were, like in other prisons, prisoners who committed themselves to the base actions of informing on their fellows, what they said and did, to the administration. Probably they were led to understand or maybe they were even made formal promises that, in exchange for the information they gave, they would be released earlier or would get other benefits.

Initially, I didn't want to believe that some of our suffering fellows accepted playing such a role; how could a former minister or a former general be capable of such a great meanness? Later I had to admit that these kind of people exist; I also saw the consequences of their actions: the "secret" was reinforced, any possibility of getting information through the window or door was cut. From the moment when he warned us about the informers, "the Aviator" became more cautious and reserved; he continued to give us information, but told us to be aware of a certain person who reported everything to the administration. Of course we assured him that we would be careful; but we had a pang, a feeling of extreme embarrassment imagining what this ordinary uncultured but honest and kind hearted man thought about the character of some former state dignitaries.

"Cireşică" was the shortest of all the wardens in the prison. He was the height of a twelve or thirteen year old, having a round childlike face. We nicknamed him "Cireşică" (little cherry). In fact, his name was Ştefan Paşcu and he was from Ţigăneştii-Criş, Bihor County: he told me that himself when I was in isolation in cell twenty-one. Being a Uniate he had a particular consideration for the Uniate priests to whom I think he gave information from outside. He also had a particular respect for Iuliu Maniu.

One day, there had been some food left in the tub – it was better food than usual – and I asked him whether I should leave it on the second floor, where he was on duty, or take it to the kitchen. He said: "Leave it here; I will give it to the man in this cell", and he pointed to the cell where Maniu was imprisoned. "Are you giving it to Iuliu Maniu?" I asked, knowing who was in that cell; "Yes" – "Cireşică" answered – "he is our father" and he held his finger to his lips, for silence.

He wasn't capable of saying harsh words or swearing. From time to time, in order to not be suspected or considered a weak and incompetent warden, he used to scream: "Move faster" but, at the same time he winked, meaning: don't take this seriously. When we asked him for news, he always answered: "Things are going well, things are going well" or "Don't worry, it's all right! You will get out of here!", but he never gave us, to those in group seventeen, precise information. I had the feeling that – in contrast to "the Aviator" – he wasn't very knowledgeable in international political issues.

It was very funny to see "Cireşică", as tiny as a child, wearing small boots and playing the big man: he would direct traffic in the hall, waving his hands, acting very serious, deepening his voice and then, when his co-workers couldn't see, turning to us and making faces and winking.

He left behind good memories; by the end of 1953, if my memory is right, he was gone. Maybe he was the victim of an informer or maybe the regime didn't trust him anymore. I don't know, but I haven't seen him since then.

"Gavrilă Pop" from Vișeul de Sus, Maramureș, was a well built, beautiful young man, with a round jaw and a pleasant voice. He used to often sing traditional Romanian songs, and well known ballads. On the night of Christmas Eve in 1950 he sung carols near my cell door. I listened to him, deeply touched, and in the morning when he opened my door I thanked him. His eyes softened; "So you heard them; you didn't sleep" "I heard all of them" – I answered – "You reminded me of the Christmas Eves' when I was free". Since then, whenever he had the occasion, he used to stand by my cell and sing or hum in a deep voice. The same man, during the first winter (1950-51), when the central heating didn't work and we had to use wood stoves for heating, used to bring me a bigger load of wood, seven pieces instead of six. When I complained that we were not given fruit and fresh vegetables -we were only given an onion now and then – he brought me, from the kitchen, raw carrots. They seemed to be a delicacy to me. Whenever I asked him about what was new, he answered like "Cireșică", "Things are going well"; in fact, he also didn't seem too interested in international politics.

"Gavrilă Pop" was the one who told me that "Here in prison is the biggest infamy". In 1951 he disappeared, I never saw him again: probably he wasn't considered appropriate for the climate in Sighet.

"Bălăcescu" was nicknamed this because he resembled Bebe Bălăcescu of the National Bank: tall and thin with a long face. I don't know whether he was Romanian or not; I would like to think that he was. He spoke with a small difficulty, but the construction of verbs and the accent and words were correct. I heard him once pronouncing the word Budapest in the Hungarian way: Boo-doh-pesh-te, but this could be explained by the fact that a large number of people in Transylvania, especially those in the north and the west, pronounced this word like the Hungarians.

Calm and polite, often helpful, he was one of the nicest wardens; it is a pity that we only had him for the last year. When I was isolated in cell sixty, during my illness, he often asked me about my health, and each morning he asked me whether I wanted extra food. When I told him that I had been imprisoned for nearly five years and that for more than two I was alone in a cell, he was surprised, almost frightened. He always addressed the prisoners in a gentlemanly way. Everything in this mans' behavior showed his natural distinction and human quality. "The mother-in-law" was also a nice warden, despite his unfavorable nickname. We named him that because he always had an observation to make; he was a little bit picky. But he didn't do it with meanness, with irony or loathing, as others did; in fact he had a good understanding soul. He used to speak in a calm voice, almost pleading: "Come on, number one (i.e. section one)" with the same tone as a headmistress in a girls' school uses to speak to her pupils.

He had an oldish, sallow face and you could see that he had had an unhappy childhood and youth. He liked everything to be clean; he used to inspect the floor thoroughly and ask: "When did you wash it last? I guess you better wash it"; he said everything very gently. He came, like "Bălăcescu", in the last period of our detention; in his first days, Victor Papacostea, wanting to make a joke, said that he knew for certain that "the mother-in-law" was a Jew and liked us because he believed that there were two Jews among us. We believed him and when "the mother-in-law" was on duty, when he opened the door one could hear, on purpose, one of the fellows telling the other: "Listen, Goldenberg, take care of your tin" or things like that; the important thing was that the warden would hear a name that sounded Jewish. After a few days, Victor told me that it was just a joke; but this game lasted for almost a month, before everyone understood that it was a joke.

"Ghiţulescu" resembled the engineer Ghiţulescu from "Mica"; therefore we nicknamed him this. Tall and solidly built, with dark hair, he was a Hungarian. He used to speak Hungarian, even at work, when he found someone who spoke it. He also spoke Romanian correctly but with an accent and some expressions that revealed his ethnic origin. It's possible that he was from Secuime[33] because he was very good at chopping wood; he probably had worked in the forests there as a wood chopper; but he also could have been from Maramureş.

Obstinate when he was upset or irritated, he gritted his teeth to

---

[33] A region in eastern Transilvania, inhabited mainly by Hungarians. (Szeklers)

control himself. He used to keep an eye on Papacostea, saying that he wasn't suffering from heart disease – as he affirmed – and that he only pretended in order to be exempt from work. One day, when I was working in the yard, "Ghițulescu" told me that he was suffering from heart disease and that, despite this, he worked as a warden twelve hours a day; I answered that in questions of illness, we shouldn't compare the free men to those who are imprisoned.

"Ghițulescu" was the warden who caused the incident with the handcuffs. Some of the fellows had the impression that he wanted to take revenge and that Bentoiu, humming the opera aria, offered him the chance. About a half an hour earlier, at Bentoiu's (who liked Romanian history) request, I had told them as a follow up to the previous lectures, about the campaign in 1330, and I'd insisted, based on the documents of that time and especially on the account from "Chronicom-pictum", upon the fight and victory at Posada. I told them how the Hungarians suffered a crushing defeat, which made Basarab the Great's, the founder of Muntenia, independence possible. My lecture about this brilliant Romanian victory made Bentoiu have an outburst of deep satisfaction, accompanied by an expression, not very agreeable, about Hungarians. The fellows affirm that "Ghițulescu", on duty that day, listened at the door to my lecture and to what Bentoiu had said, and that being a Hungarian he was angry but didn't want to intervene him-self, so he waited for the reason to satisfy his desire for revenge. In this way, my fellows explained, his persistence in involving me by accusing me of also singing was clear. Such an explanation could be true. However, I have to say that "Ghițulescu" didn't need to wait for an opportunity but could have easily reported that we had proved nationalism and tried to create enmity between Romanians and Hungarians. Actually, it wouldn't have been the first lie that the wardens had told about us. We didn't think for a moment, neither my fellows or I, about such a thing. I'd rather explain the wardens' gesture as his desire to be noticed, to prove that he was vigilant, to win – ambitious as he was – a new promotion. A few days earlier we had been told that it was forbidden to sing and the man thought that he had the chance to report a case of rule breaking to the administration. Another proof that he wanted to be noticed at any price was that he applied, literally, the new directors' orders concerning the supervision of the prisoners in the cells: he walked, day and night, when he was on duty, along the cells and inspected each cell every two minutes. If you do that for twelve hours a day it becomes exhausting. However, "Ghiţulescu" did it like a robot.

"Nazone", nicknamed after his extraordinarily large nose – the biggest in the prison – was almost as tall as "Păsărilă". He had a purplish complexion, which was another distinctive feature of his.

He liked to talk dirty. On one of my sleepless nights, I heard a long conversation between him and "Boca", recently married; 'Boccacio' could have found rich inspiring material in this conversation.

Sometimes, he didn't hesitate to hit the prisoners: he was one of the four wardens who beat me one midnight when I was alone in cell twenty-one. I heard that he also beat others. On the other hand he also had good points. Many times, in the autumn of 1950, he brought me an extra portion of corn meal, and he hid it under my pillow so it wouldn't be seen by another warden. When I told him that I had no news from my family – which depressed me a lot – and that I didn't think I'd be released soon, he always said: "Here in prison you must have courage; if you don't have courage you're screwed; even those who are sentenced to death still must have courage, because you never know...".

At the very beginning, in the end of June or beginning of July of 1950, he asked me whether my name was Gheorghescu and whether I was a professor. I had the feeling that someone in the town made him get information about me.

The Security Officers

In the beginning, "the Mute"; a Sub-Lieutenant with a livid, blueish face; he used to say that he suffered from all the diseases we said we had ("Me too!").

"Tuberculosis": was short and mean. He looked for spies among us and eventually he found them; the third security officer was "Gorilla" or "Gore"; he was a physical degenerate. He established *the frog* and *the bustard*, "Neagra" was used at its' maximum because of him. In November of 1953 a fourth security officer came "Martel", a Lieutenant-Major, with three stars on his lapel (from that comes his nickname) while his predecessors had only been Sub-Lieutenants. He tightened measures concerning "the secret" in order that we not communicate with each other and not get news from outside, and generally he succeeded. His method was: "Suaviter in modo, fortiter in re"; individual conversations in his office; collective conversations in the cells; the last significant conversations, in May 1955. The last security officer was again a Sub-Lieutenant, gypsy looking and with a bad, worrying look. He took our fingerprints.

The inspections and inquests

During the five years and two months we had a whole series of inspections and inquests. The inspections were administrative and the inquiries were for form, with the exception of around three of them and especially the last, which was the most important. The last took three months and concerned substance, not only form.

In 1955, the inspections were successive over a short interval of time, for the first time there was the *prosecutor* who asked us persistently whether we had anything to tell him in confidence; the inquest concerning the hard currency, precious metals and jewels; the inquest concerning the relations with other countries and the foreign diplomatic corp. We were asked thirteen or fourteen times who our parents were, brothers and sisters, what possessions we had etc.

The Black Cell ("Neagra")

There was a "Neagra"(the black cell) on the second floor and one on the third floor (cell thirty-nine was the last to the left on the second floor; cell sixty-nine was on the third floor).

I stayed there seven times, alone, and one time with the fellows in group eighteen. Here Cămărăşescu caught a cold; here Aurelian Bentoiu stayed handcuffed in June of 1955; Mihalache stayed here *several months*, with the feces container which was changed only once a week.

In 1953, after the food had become better, "Neagra" was disused. However, in June of 1955, Bentoiu was put there.

There was also a cell called "Sura" (gray room): a room on the third floor which didn't have a direct window, only a small window looking into the corridor, so that it received little light. Here, Ilie Lazăr was put for many months. He had an emaciated, pale face, with eyes which shone like he was sick with fever. He used to pull himself up on the bars to the high window and ask for or give news.

Other punishments. Besides "Neagra", there were also other punishments: "the frog", "the bustard", the kneeling, the denial of food or its' reduction in one or many meals. Then there was the *beating*, which was often used during the first few years. Who have been beaten: V. Slăvescu, Sever Dan, I. Lupaş, M. Romaşcanu, A. Bentoiu, Victor Papacostea, C. Zamfirescu and many others.

The communication and the news in prison

We were not allowed to read anything (neither books nor magazines nor newspapers); no communication was allowed with your family; we didn't have a pen, pencil and paper; we had nothing which could facilitate contact with the outside or with our fellow prisoners in Sighet.

However, we were able to establish contact, first with our fellow prisoners, then through some of them, even with the outside.

With our fellow prisoners we had contact through the window or door, during the "walk" or work in the yard and during the corridor cleaning. How I communicated: the contact with Cornățeanu, Sibiceanu, Victor Papacostea, Nistor, Aug. Filip, Zamfirescu etc., through the window. Contact through the door with the priests, in the morning, during the sweeping and then the floor washing. Communication by notes left in the ashes in the boiler room or the kitchen; the error made by Zamfirescu: during the search they found notes on him concerning his conversation with a sentinel who used to give them – those in group seventeen – cigarettes and even newspapers; the wretched soldier was severely punished, maybe even shot. It seems that after this the "Mute" was replaced with "Tuberculosis".

The communication through the walls, with the neighbor nearest on either side, was the classic way of knocking and tap-ping. In this way, I communicated for a long time with Coriolan Băran who was in cell twenty-two. I also communicated through the wall with Sibiceanu, who remained in group seventeen, while another four prisoners from this group were moved to group eighteen.

The system was simple: for the first letter of the alphabet, "A", a knock; for "B" two knocks; for "C", three knocks and so on, with the "Z" communicated by twenty-five knocks. It is easy to understand how long it took, under these conditions, to transmit a sentence made of a few words. Therefore, we adopted abbreviations. After each word, two short knocks; we had the call code: three long knocks and a short one (letter "V" in Morse code; the radio signal during the war); the danger code: three pounds with the fist. There was another system which I didn't use.

We used to communicate, preferably in the morning after we got the news from the kitchen team or immediately after lunch when the supervision was lax. Often, we also communicated after the roll call, when the wardens were not so vigilant.

Cleaning

For the prisoners cleaning was an occasion for unpleasant work and humiliation. There were different systems for cleaning the floors of halls and corridors: the "moon and bulb", "I want to see sparks", etc.

Every morning we had to clean the toilets, some of them being flooded with water which we had to evacuate. During the first days, we didn't have feces containers in the cells – those who were alone in the cells, at least – and were taken three times a day -in the morning, at noon and in the evening – to the toilet where we were allowed to spend a minute or two. Only after two weeks were we given an empty can and after another two weeks we were given a feces container made of oak wood.

The cleaning of the toilets was done with hands in urine, using some dirty rags. Boca took a sadistic pleasure in making us clean the toilets.

The sewers were cleaned by us as well. Dumitru Nistor was forced to get into the sewer and take out the filth with buckets that his cell-mates carried further; when he came out of the sewer he had filth all over his body. In 1954, on St. Constantine's Day, we cleaned the sewers again; they were getting clogged often; this time I was one of those who carried the buckets. We had to empty these buckets, despite our protests and opposition, into the garbage trench in the yard near the watch-tower. We warned that in this way the place would be infected by germs and an epidemic could arise. The stupid section head didn't listen to us and he forced us to empty them there. Several days later everyone in the prison was concerned; there was a rumor of an epidemic, typhoid fever; the doctor was absent for two months and we found out that there was a serious typhus epidemic in the region and in the rest of the country. We reported that we had warned the section head that it wasn't a good thing to put the fecal matter there and that he didn't pay attention to what we'd said. I believe that the section head was punished; also serious measures were taken for cleaning and disinfecting.

The market in Sighet Penitentiary

There was a food exchange: meat for marmalade, milk for bread, etc. You could sell the privilege of being the first to chose the meat. The expert was Romaşcanu who used to buy and sell everything; this was also an opportunity for fun and jokes (Sibiceanu).

Lectures

In every inmates group there were organized lectures on subjects like History, Literature, Science, Law, Religion, etc. The most appreciated were the lectures on History and Literature. On the occasion of these lectures we had real revelations: for example we realized that Miluță Romaşcanu had a storytelling talent (He spoke of memories from his youth and childhood: the villages Plugari and Zlătunoaia in Iaşi and Botoşani Counties, where he spent his childhood, then Iaşi after the first world war, then Bucharest between 1925-30).

We also realized that Aurelian Bentoiu had a gift for poetry. He is not only a remarkable lawyer – maybe the most efficient in Bucharest – but he also has a real talent for poetry.

In inmate group seventeen the conference holders were: Victor Papacostea, N. Sibiceanu, N. Cornăţeanu, M. Romaşcanu, Gen. N. Marinescu, G. Strat, Dumitru Nistor and my self. I. Ştefănescu Goangă and Ion Nistor held lectures in inmate group eighteen.

List of Lectures held in Sighet Penitentiary

I Myself: History, Geography, Historical Geography, Literature, Science, and Miscellaneous.

1) History:

a) *General course in History of Romanians*, part 1 (from the pre-history to the military organization of Roman Dacia: thirty-five lectures) – inmate group thirteen

b) *Foreign travelers in Romanian Provinces*, (twenty-five lectures) – inmate group eighteen

c) *The history of Bucharest*, from the oldest times to current days (nine lectures) – inmate group seventeen

d) *The history of Curtea de Argeş*, from oldest times to current days (four lectures) – inmate group eighteen

e) *The history of the town Callatis – Mangalia*, from oldest times to current days (four lectures) – inmate group seventeen

f) *Stephan The Great* in the light of the newly discovered historical sources (two lectures) inmate group seventeen

g) *Mircea the Old*, (two lectures) inmate group seventeen

h) *Petru Rareş*, (two lectures) inmate group seventeen

i) *Basarab the Great and the founding of Wallachia*, (three lectures) inmate groups seventeen and eighteen

j) *Flowers and Gardens in our past*, (one lecture) inmate group seventeen

k) *Pilgrims and Pilgrimages in our past*, (one lecture) inmate group thirteen

l) *Surcouf, the French Buccaneer*, (one lecture) inmate group eighteen

m) *Alexandru Lăpuşneanu*, (one lecture) inmate group eighteen

n) *Fishing and Fish Hatcheries in our past*, (four lectures) inmate group seventeen

o) *January 24th 1859*, (one lecture) inmate group seventeen

p) *May 10th 1877*, (one lecture) inmate group seventeen

q) *The Founding of Moldavia*, (two lectures) inmate group seventeen

r) *My biography*, (twenty lectures) inmate group eighteen

2) Geography and Historical Geography

a) *A journey around the world by boat*, (thirty-five lectures) inmate group seventeen

b) *Cities and Nations in the Soviet Union*, (four lectures) inmate group seventeen

c) *Putna County*, (five lectures) inmate group seventeen

d) *Ilfov County*, (four lectures) inmate group seventeen

e) *Tulcea County*, (two lectures) inmate group seventeen

f) *Croisiere Blanche*, (two lectures) inmate group seventeen

g) *Nous avons fait un beau voyage* by Francis De Croisset (four lectures) (India and Ceylon) – inmate group thirteen

h) *The journey of three American aviators in the Pacific in a rubber boat for 36 days* (after "Readers Digest") (two lectures) inmate group seventeen

i) *Press Report on Laponia* (after "Life" magazine) (one lecture) inmate group seventeen

j) *Istanbul* (description made by me) (five lectures) inmate group seventeen

k) *Egypt* (description made by me) (five lectures) inmate group seventeen

3) Literature
a) *Le Roman de Tristan et Iseut* (from the modern version by Bédier) (three lectures) inmate group seventeen
b) *The Christ's Shirt*, a novel by Lloyd Douglas (one lecture) inmate group seventeen
c) *Maria Chappedelaine*, a novel by Louis Hemon (two lectures) inmate group seventeen
d) *Captains' Courageous*, by Rudyard Kipling (three lectures) inmate group seventeen
e) *Pirin Planina*, by G. Topârceanu (four lectures) inmate group seventeen
f) *Fraţii Jderi* (The brothers Jderi), by M. Sadoveanu (eight sessions) inmate group seventeen
g) *Zodia Cancerului* (The sign of Cancer), by M. Sadoveanu (four sessions) inmate group seventeen
h) *Nunta Domniţei Ruxandra* (The wedding of Princess Ruxandra), by M. Sadoveanu (three sessions) inmate group seventeen
i) *Une descente dans le Maelstrom*, by Egdar Allan Poe (one session) inmate group seventeen
j) *El Hakim*, by John Knittel, (two sessions) inmate group seventeen

4) Science and Miscellaneous
a) *Le Ciel*, (one lecture) inmate group seventeen
b) *Lady Hamilton*, a film I saw in Istanbul – inmate group thirteen

I also whistled and sang old Romanian songs, the "Doina", "Romance", Italian Canzonettas, etc.

II Aurelian Bentoiu

a) *Poems* by himself (ten lectures that were repeated later) – inmate groups eighteen and fifty-nine
b) *"Skoda" case* (five lectures) inmate group eighteen
c) *Different cases* he pleaded (for example, the case of peasants who owned oil rich land) – inmate group eighteen
d) *The definition and evolution of Law*, (ten lectures) inmate group eighteen; he also spoke of this subject in inmate group fifty-nine.

III Victor Papacostea

a) *The History of the Romanians in the Balkans*, (twelve to fifteen lectures) inmate group seventeen
b) *The enemies of Rome*, (Mitridate, Jugurtha, Hannibal, Decebal) (twelve to fifteen lectures) inmate group seventeen
c) *The development of Romanian Historiography*, (I didn't attend these lectures) inmate group seventeen
d) *Constantin Giurescu*, (two lectures) inmate group seventeen
e) *Moscopole*, (four to five lectures) inmate group seventeen
f) *My childhood district in Bucharest*, (11 June, Blvd. Mărășești, Bellu) (eight lectures) inmate group seventeen
g) *Autobiography*, (four lectures) inmate group eighteen (attended by Nae Marinescu, G. Leon and myself)
h) *Mihai Viteazul (Mihai the Brave)*, in Romanian Historiography (four to five lectures) inmate group seventeen
i) *Foreign travelers in our Provinces*, in the beginning of the 19th Century (between 1806-21) (eight lectures) inmate group eighteen
j) *The Cadrilater*, (three to four lectures) inmate group thirteen
k) *Quo Vadis*, by H. Szienkiewicz (four lectures) inmate group seventeen
l) *Through Fire and Sword*, by H. Szienkiewicz (four lectures) inmate group seventeen
m) *Les Misérables*, by Victor Hugo (five to six lectures) inmate group seventeen
n) *The Deluge*, by H. Szienkiewicz (four lectures) inmate group seventeen

He also whistled arias from operas, serenades, lullabies, etc.; he used to tell film plots (Colonel Blicup; The last of the Mohicans; People burned at the Stake, etc.)

IV Nicu Sibiceanu

a) *My journey to Istanbul and Ankara*, (one lecture) inmate group seventeen
b) *The journey to Belgrade*, (one lecture) inmate group seventeen
c) *The journey to Prague*, (one lecture) inmate group seventeen
He made these journeys when he was Cabinet Director of Gh. Tătărăscu.

d) *Gone with the Wind*, by Margaret Mitchell (ten lectures) inmate groups seventeen and eighteen

e) *Röpke*, by himself (one lecture) inmate group seventeen

f) *The bridges of Paris*, (one lecture) inmate group seventeen

Language Training

Besides lectures there was also language training. I learned Hungarian from Dumitru Nistor; during the next period, Aurelian Bentoiu learned Hungarian with me. He also had learned earlier from Aurel Vlad. Dumitru Nistor learned French and English from Nicu Sibiceanu. Sibiceanu, Cornăţeanu, Strat and myself practiced our English together.

When I was in Cornăţeanu's' group I practiced my French and English with the fellows and also refreshed my knowledge of German together with Victor Moldovan.

When I was alone in the cell, between May of 1950 and January of 1952 and October of 1954 to February of 1955, I reviewed my knowledge of English, German and Latin. I also reviewed my knowledge of History and World Geography. I concentrated upon formulating *new scientific works*, namely:

Volume four of *The History of Romanians* (Part 1: Politics and Part 2: Institutions and Culture)

– *The History of Bucharest*

– *Fishing and Fish Hatcheries in our past*

– A series of articles in History, Geography, Cartography, Archeology, Philology and Bibliography; about 260 articles

– The translation of *The History of Romanians*, a resume based on the Delafras edition, in French, German, English, Italian, Spanish, Greek, Serbian, Bulgarian and Turkish, each translation having new information about the respective people. The titles will be something like *The History of Romanians with emphasis on their relationship with the Greeks* or *The History of Romanians and their relationship with the Bulgarians* etc.

These scientific preoccupation were very useful to me; they helped me pass the time, especially when I was alone in the cell, and helped me to keep my memory intact and even improve and stimulate it.

Thinking of Mica and the children, whom I really wanted to see again, and having these scientific preoccupations allowed me to resist and get out alive from the horrible Sighet prison.

I also thought of making a volume with the oldest and best

Romanian songs, beginning with those mentioned in the Veréss Romanian-Hungarian bibliography and in St. Bellanger, Le Kéroutza.

Another work – *Unpublished documents concerning the borders between Transylvania and the Principalities in the 18th Century* – will include documents that my father found and copied in Vienna, and it is a continuation of the work *Materials for the History of Oltenia under Austrian rule.* Another one – *Unpublished Romanian Documents concerning the relationship between Muntenia and Athos Mountain* – will include the materials that have been entrusted to me by Gabriel Millet from Paris and is a continuation of Grigore Nandriş's *Documents...* published in the historical section of the publishing house of the Royal Foundations.

ADDENDA

The Chronology of my Detention
(The cells I stayed in)

– May 6, 1950: The arrest
– May 7, 1950: The arrival in Sighet and my imprisonment in cell number twenty-one
– December 1950: I stay in cell number ten, then return to cell number twenty-one
– June 1951: Again in cell number ten, then I return to cell number twenty-one
– Jan. 25, 1952: Transferred to cell number forty-eight (Cornăţeanu's inmate group)
– Feb. 26, 1952: Transferred to the kitchen team (cell number seventeen)
– June 27, 1953: Removed from kitchen duty
– December 1953 – February 1954: Transferred (the four of us) to cell number eighteen (next to cell seventeen)
– March 1954: We are returned to cell seventeen
– April 1954: We are all transferred to cell thirteen
– Sept. 24, 1954: Regrouping of the liberals (ten people) and the return to cell eighteen
– Oct. 13, 1954: Because I am sick I am moved to cell sixty (second floor)
– Feb. 7, 1955: I return to inmate group eighteen
– July 5, 1955: I am released from the prison; I have mandatory domicile for 60 months in Măzăreni

Addenda et corrigenda (Măzăreni)

– Engineer Priboianu told me today, Sept. 5, 1955, (in *Măzăreni*) that he thinks that C. Argetoianu died in cell number twelve, next to the cell where he stayed with A. Filip and with the others from the pump group (number thirteen), on January 27, Argetoianu's birthday.

After Argetoianu a priest was moved to cell number twelve. He communicated with them through the wall and told them he was a priest. After this priest another priest stayed there and in April engineer Priboianu himself was moved to cell number twelve and stayed there until July 5th when he was released.

August Filip cried a lot when Argetoianu died (Gh. Strat told me, on this occasion, that there was a rumor in Bucharest that A. Filip was the natural son of Argetoianu).

I knew that Argetoianu died in the first days of February of 1955. When I returned to inmate group eighteen, on Feb. 7, 1955, I saw that they were cleaning cell number twelve and my fellows (Sibiceanu, Victor Papacostea, Nistor, Bentoiu) told me that Argetoianu died there. *In any case, Argetoianu's death happened between Jan. 26 and Feb. 6 of 1955.*

The same Priboianu told me today, Sept. 7, 1955, that he saw generals *Sova and Iacobici* in Sighet, in the prison yard in November and December of 1954. These two generals were considered "War Criminals" by the authorities. They were his friends and he knew them very well. I asked him twice if they were really them, if he had seen them well and was sure, and *he confirmed this strongly.* Gh. Strat was with us, and he told me that he didn't know anything about the presence of the two generals in Sighet. Were they really in Sighet?

Niculescu-Buzești, the brother of the former foreign Minister, *Camil Demetrescu* and *Victor Rădulescu-Pogoneanu* also were in Sighet. They stayed on the first floor in cell number thirteen or fourteen.

– Priboianu told me, Gh. Strat being present on Sept. 19, the following: "Cireșică" was named by them "Piticot" (the dwarf); "Habsburg" was called "The hysterical"; "Tuberculosis" was called "Fish".

Bornemisa was an *informer*. He said that *"he'll do anything to get out"* (this is the exact declaration made to us by G. Leon!).

He told the fellows in his group that he would make the speeches during the roll call on communist holidays (March 6th, May 1st, etc.). And he did it; he did it so persistently and subserviently that the Lieutenant (Biaritz) interrupted him, saying: "Enough, I've had this up to here..."

Priboianu thinks that he died of *cancer*! He was isolated during the last period of his detention; when they took him out of the group, in order to play his role he told his fellows; "I'm going to take care of some old people".

After they isolated him, he was seen in the yard sitting on the stones of the old fountain. His tumor that they had operated on in prison had grown back; when they put him under anesthetic the doctor ("the Frog") and Benzo were there; when he awoke there was only Benzo! (The scene with "the Barber" where Bornemisa was interrogated by "Tuberculosis").

Racoviţă-Jandarmul was an *informer* too; when he returned from the interrogation he said: "I think I didn't frame anyone in this room" (so he did frame people from other rooms).

He had a servile, very humble, even undignified attitude towards the prison staff. He was filthy and didn't want to work at all, he used to spit and piss on the floor that others had scrubbed and washed.

I. Nistor used to carry the feces container when he was in cell fifty-nine; when he was moved to our cell he didn't want to do any work; he was revolted that Racoviţă didn't work at all!

Gh. Strat specified that our transfer from cell number thirteen to cell eighteen and the addition of another four liberals from cell fifty-nine was done on *Sept. 29, 1954. I think he was correct!*

I was moved (isolated) to cell sixty on Oct. 13, 1954 and returned on Feb. 7, 1955.

Gh. Strat had his crisis of urine retention and nervous spasms on April 19, 1955. (I specified this date and he agreed!)

Priboianu told me that Zwiedenek had received two suitcases filled with documents from Queen Maria that he was supposed to send to Germany after her death; he kept postponing this, although he could have sent them during Antonescu's regime; eventually, under the communists, during a search, the police found the suitcases. While he was in Priboianu's group, Zwiedenek used to kneel on the floor and beat his head, blaming himself for the mistake he'd made by not sending the documents. They are now in the hands of communists.

– Solomon told me today, Oct. 1, 1955, at Priboianu's place, Gh. Strat, Priboianu and Vlad Dimitriu being present, the following things about Sighet:

He, Solomon, together with Mihai Popovici, Mihail Manoilescu and Radu Budișteanu arrived in Sighet on Nov. 12, 1950 at 11 p.m. After spending the night in cell number thirteen on the ground floor, they were moved to cell number sixty-seven ("the gray room"), above the medics' room (the so called "sick room").

There, in room sixty-seven, Mihail Manoilescu died on the night of Dec. 30-31, 1950. He had contracted exanthematic typhus when he was arrested; he escaped the typhus but his heart was damaged. In Sighet he died of heart and kidney failure, as a consequence of the typhus.

Pufi Leucuția arrived in Sighet later, in 1954; therefore we didn't see him and didn't know about him.

On Sept. 29, 1954 Solomon, together with C. Angelescu, C. Băran, Tomescu, Aug. Filip, Priboianu and Voicu Nițescu were brought to room number thirteen where they found Cornățeanu and R. Pop from our former group. They worked at the pump (Voicu Nițescu didn't work, Solomon only half worked, etc.; those who really worked were Cornățeanu, Pop, Băran; and Tomescu was half valid).

In January of 1955 R. Pop was isolated after he had been interrogated several times about three women from Oradea who had crossed the border and left the country. Solomon was also interrogated about these women. One of the women was the head of the feminine section of the party in Oradea.

On April 1, 1955 Priboianu, Voicu Nițescu, Solomon and C. Angelescu were separated and moved into single cells on the ground floor (cells eleven, twelve, twenty and twenty-one). They stayed there until their release. In cell thirteen Cornățeanu, Băran, Filip and Tomescu remained.

I. Mihalache left Sighet on Nov. 17, 1953 together with nine other prisoners.

Solomon asserted that *in Sighet* he met the hardest regime of all the prisons he'd been in! And he was in many prisons: at the Ministry of the Interior, in Jilava, in Pitești, in Aiud and in Ocnele Mari. When he arrived in Sighet he was very ill. His pulse rate was 200.

Solomon also stayed in cell eighty-eight on the third floor, being neighbors with Dumitru Alimănişteanu who was in cell eighty-seven (next to the toilet)! The latter talked to him through the hole of the heating pipe: the heater wasn't repaired at that time. ("Hello, who's there; hello, who's there?")

(Măzăreni, October 1, 1955, 8 p.m.)

Room number seventy-four was above room number forty-four. Solomon spent a short time in room seventy-four too.

For *six weeks* they didn't go out for the walk! (Priboianu dixit!)

– On Oct. 12, when she came to see me in Măzăreni, Mica told me that D.V. Ţoni had died in Bucharest and that a lot of people, among them D.R. Ioaniţescu, came to the funeral.

– Mica told me on Oct. 23, when she came to Măzăreni again, that the following people had died in Bucharest:

Gen. Ilasievici, in the Malmaison Prison; he was very weak.

August Filip – who killed himself, drowning in either Lake Băneasa or Herăstrău. He had been released from Malmaison and went to a relatives' house and called his wife. She came to him and told him that during his imprisonment, for more than five years, she suffered because of the secret police and other persecutors and she didn't want to live with him anymore; meanwhile, she had gotten a divorce. A. Filip left his relatives' house – although some of his nephews who were there invited him to stay with them – and wrote, on a piece of paper, the address and telephone number of his relative. Then he took a tram, despite the nephews insistence, and went to the lake and killed himself. The nephews wanted to take the tram with him but they missed the tram.

His former wife had the lack of sense to come to the funeral. She wore a small hat on the top of her curly head. Nobody who attended the funeral – about one hundred people – would shake hands with her. This was one of the tragedies generated by Sighet!

Nolica, Tătărăscu's wife killed herself and the wife of Theology Professor Tomescu died of heart failure three days after he returned to Bucharest.

– Today, Oct. 13, 1955, Gh. Strat told me:

D. Teodorescu (Malacu) was kept in "Neagra" for two days and two nights and beaten for some raw potatoes (he had hoarded and then dropped them).

They beat *Valer Moldovan*, 78 years old, because he had stood on tiptoe to see the time on the church clock (he was in cell seventy-four together with Strat).

A. Baciu was beaten; he died in December of 1953 (at the beginning of winter at about the same time as Bădulescu).

Cudalbu also was in Sighet (C. Angelescu told Gh. Strat); he died there.

– I remembered that: Among the Uniate Prelates there was the Canon Macovei, in the group of Bishops.

The Uniate priest Berîndă was an assumptionist, like Father Laurent. I spoke to him through the door and through the window.

– Today Oct. 27, 1955, C.C. Zamfirescu was brought to me in Măzăreni by the head of the local police and was left with me with the promise that in the afternoon they would find a house for him. I gave him tea with butter and honey, then I had lunch together with him and Mica (fried eggs with corn porridge, creamed cheese and apple pie). He was sick; he had serious colitis; in the afternoon Gh. Strat came and the three of us agreed that we should take him to the local dispensary and then to the hospital in Brăila. We did it in the afternoon. I and Strat brought him the luggage that he had left with me.

During the morning and over lunch he told us that he, together with Cornățeanu and a group left Sighet on July 6, 1955 in the morning, in a prison railway car to Bucharest, and they were imprisoned in Malmaison where they stayed until they were released one by one (however, not all of them!). Zamfirescu was interrogated twenty-six times, seventeen times about himself and nine times about others. He made nine biographies of other people, among them was Victor Papacostea.

They stayed in individual, separate cells in Malmaison; the food was acceptable (two courses); he was given diet food because of his colitis. They released him last Friday; he went home and after four days, on the pretext of wanting to give him back his valuables (wedding ring, etc.), they called him to the police station and told him that he must establish mandatory domicile for sixty months in Măzăreni. He left in the evening on Wednesday, he arrived in Brăila, spent the night at the police station and arrived in Măzăreni Thursday morning.

Zamfirescu believes that Gh. Brătianu didn't kill himself but died of tuberculosis. He says he didn't see Brătianu in the yard for two weeks before he died; in reality, we, those in cell seventeen, saw

Gheorghe Brătianu in the yard just before he killed himself, on the afternoon of April 24, 1953. Zamfirescu is misinformed or maybe he doesn't want to admit that he knows that Brătianu killed himself, probably for political reasons.

– Today, Oct. 28, 1955, when I visited C.C. Zamfirescu in the Măzăreni dispensary he told me:

They were moved on Sept. 29, 1954 downstairs in group seventeen. He stayed there with Gh. Vântu, Mihai Popovici, Vasile Sassu, Lupaș, Meteș and others.

Gh. Vântu was *unrecognizable*. From 190 pounds he had gone down to *110* pounds; he was bent at the waist almost to a 90 degree angle; he had a spine ailment and intestinal disease; his rectum was about two inches outside his body. Zamfirescu didn't realize it was him; it was necessary for Vântu to tell him his name in order to be recognized.

Meteș was released first, on May 19, 1955; Lupaș about twenty days later, around the beginning of June.

Mihai Popovici had a *serious brawl* with V. Sassu because of a blanket. Popovici had prison blanket and two of his own; Sassu had two prison blankets and one of his own. When the warden came to ask for a blanket for the bathroom neither of them answered. When Popovici turned his back to them Sassu pointed to the blanket on Popovici's bed, hinting that that one should be taken, and the warden took it. But Popovici saw him when he pointed at the blanket. When the warden left, Popovici began to pace angrily in the cell and said: "Scoundrels... scoundrels... informers". Then...(see note on October 29th)

(We were interrupted by Gh. Strat's arrival!)

– Today, October 29 the, C.C. Zamfirescu told me:

Together with him on the same prison railway car came: Pufi Leucuția, Ion Mihalache, I.C. Petrescu, the last two in a separate cell; N. Zigre, Gh. Vântu and Ionel Periețianu, all three seriously ill, hardly able to move; also Ion Gigurtu, N. Cornățeanu, Sauciuc-Săveanu, Victor Papacostea, Bentoiu, D. Nistor, Mironescu-Mera and others.

Valer Moldovan, who was in inmate group seventy-four, died in Sighet in cell eighty-seven. Zamfirescu cleaned the room after he died. It happened in 1954, before September 29th when Zamfirescu was transferred downstairs, from group seventy-eight to group seventeen.

Iuliu Moldovan was also very ill; at the end he couldn't eat anything but potatoes.

Mihai Popovici slapped V. Sassu and kicked him, Titus Popovici tried to separate them and he got punched himself. Sassu was stunned, he didn't fight back (see note from October 28th).

Victor Țoni was operated on for a hernia; he died of uremia, according to Gigi Solomon who also came to visit Zamfirescu; the latter believes that he died because of an infection. I think that Solomon is right!

Gen. Ilcuș didn't die, Zamfirescu says; he came to Bucharest with the others. He wasn't insane; he pretended to be insane in order to be given a cellmate and they gave him a priest; but we heard how they beat him.

– On Sunday, Dec. 25, 1955, Ion Lupaș told me at my house:

Ion Popp (Enci Popp) died on March 9, 1953. He suddenly felt bad when he was in the barbers room; when he went to the tap to wash himself, he had an attack and fell down. He died quickly and painlessly.

Aurel Vlad died on the morning of July 1, 1953 at 3:00. He had been an atheist (although he often represented ecclesiastic institutions and forums); in his last hours he made a gesture of faith: he said 'The Lord's Prayer' (Aurelian Bentoiu told me the same thing in Sighet).

Ion Lupaș was badly beaten because he went on a hunger strike. While they were beating him, Lupaș screamed: "Hit me in the head so you can finish me". The warden who was beating him answered: "I will do that at the end". Lupaș had to give up his hunger strike; otherwise they would have beaten him to death.

He ascertained that, like with me, his memory improved in prison because of continually exercising it.

G. Tașcă died of pneumonia, probably, in 1951. He used to lament alone in the night in his Moldavian dialect: "Văleu, Mămucă, Văleu" (Alas, mother, alas). Necșești, who stayed close to his cell, heard him.

The Dead

They started to die on their way to the prison; Dr. Ciugureanu died in Turda (May 6, 1950).

Gen. Cihoski went crazy during the journey; he died a short time after his arrival in Sighet.

Popovici-Taşcă Popovici-T.

The death of Gen. Popovici-Epure: his sickness and recovery; the final numbing attack. The scene of his removal from the cell!

The death of Engineer Macovei, of heart failure.

The death of Măgureanu: his last will.

The death of Al. Lapedatu: he hung himself.

The suicide of Radu Roşculeţ.

The suicide of Gh. Brătianu: he cut his throat.

The suicide of Costel Tătăreanu; his liver disease.

How Bishop Suciu died.

The death of Dinu Brătianu, etc.

How were the dead buried? In coffins at the beginning; then without coffins, carried with blankets. The midnight cart: the sound of the body thrown into the cart. The sinister stretcher; the spades loaded with dirt. The undertaker: the barber. The medic performed autopsies before coming to Sighet and probably continued to do that in prison. It would be interesting to see what death certificates were issued in prison and how they labeled the suicides. The belongings of the dead were taken partly by their cellmates and partly by the administration.

How we verified someone's death: By the number of pieces of bread cut in the kitchen and by the fact that the tubs of food didn't stop at that respective cell.

Ion Pelivan passed away on December 24, 1953; he was sick for a long time and, although the doctor (the young one who replaced the "frog") prescribed injections of penicillin for him, he was only given an *aspirin*! The medic who was *in charge* didn't want to give him injections!

D. Burilleanu, former governor of the National Romanian Bank, died exactly four months after Pelivan, i.e. on April 24, 1954. He also was ill; in the last stages of his illness he couldn't eat anything; he couldn't even tolerate bread soaked in water, he threw up immediately. He must have had *stomach cancer* like poor Dorel Dumitrescu. And like the latter, *he didn't have any pain*, he didn't suffer like those who have cancer usually do.

(Details given today, August 8, 1955, in the morning, in Măzăreni, by Engineer Priboianu who stayed in the same cell with both of them!)

Bentoiu told me in Sighet that he was a witness to the deaths of Enci Pop and Aurel Vlad. The latter was an *atheist*, but before he died he accepted last rites. One of them died on June 30, 1953 (Aurel Vlad, I think!); the other seems to have died on Martyrs' Day (March 9).

Cornățeanu knows when Macovei and Gen. Popovici-Epure died (they both died between October of 1950 and March of 1951).

Miluță Romașcanu witnessed Măgureanu's death and knows his last wishes. (I think it also was at the beginning of 1951!).

Ștefănescu-Goangă was in the inmate group where Burilleanu and Pelivan died. Gen. Racoviță-Jandarmul died in cell number seventeen, alone, of skin cancer when he was 88 years old, in 1954.

Remarkable Facts

(In connection with animals): 1 – *The spider* with a cross on its' back, in my cell (number twenty-one) who kept me company for two months in the summer of 1951; she became tame; she knew me. 2 – The prison's *puppy*, given to the dogcatchers by the prison director personally; he was looking for our affection. 3 – *Leul* (the lion), the big dog who used to play with us and bark desperately at the sentinels (the brutality of "Păsărilă"); he was especially mine and Cornățeanu's friend. 4 -*The cat* in the kitchen that they dropped from the wall. 5 – *The eaglet* who fell – it was probably sick – in September of 1954, into the prison yard; the director brought it into our cell (number thirteen): a splendid bird (description!). We kept it *in the toilet!* The wardens used to bother it. It was shot by a sentinel and died, it seems, like Ilie from Buzău (Ilie, the eagle from Buzău!) 6 – *The swallow* that fell between the two panels of the front window and died after trying unsuccessfully to get out for four days. 7 – *The rats*; the rat hunting; the scene with the female rat who stayed to protect her babies and died: example of maternal sacrifice. Leul used to take part in the rat hunting. 8 – *The mice* in the kitchen, friends of Miluță Romașcanu who rescued them when they fell into an empty kettle: he used to put pieces of wood down for them to climb out of the kettle on; on the other hand, Gen. Nae Marinescu used to throw them into the fire alive. 9 – *The pigs* (*"Ghiță" and "Marița"!*); their food; Marița's piglets, midwived by Cornățeanu and Miluță Romașcanu; later I helped them myself. The slaughtering of Ghiță and Marița's' fear. Romașcanu used to take care of their food. The bucket, its' sound made Marița squeal immediately. "Dați la oi" and pigs food! 10 – *The crows* who searched the sparrows' nests' and ate their babies; repeated scenes of this kind seen from cell thirteen. 11 – *The owls* who sang especially in the autumn. 12 – *The Cuckoo*, in spring, especially in the spring of 1951 and 1955 (it sang very early in the morning, at about 4 a.m.!) 13 – *The wild geese*. They left in the autumn and returned in the spring. One evening, between 8:30 and 11:00, I counted twelve flocks). 14 – *The hoopoe*; I heard it a few times...

ANNEXES

by
Lia Ioana Ciplea

APPENDIX 1

THE LIST OF DIGNITARIES WHO DIED IN SIGHET BETWEEN MAY 6, 1950 AND JULY 5, 1955

Argetoianu, Constantin (1871-1955)

Ph.D. in Medicine, degree in Law and Literature (Paris)

Enters diplomatic service in 1898 – Secretary and Counselor of the Romanian Diplomatic mission in Vienna

Member of the Conservative Party

Senator (1914)

Minister of Justice (1918), Minister of Finance (1920) and Minister of the Interior (1920-21) in the Averescu government.

Ad Interim Minister for Agriculture and for Internal Affairs (1927) in the Barbu Știrbey government

Minister of Agriculture and Domains (1927-28) in the I.C. Brătianu government

Finance Minister (1931-32), also ad interim Minister for Foreign Affairs (1931) and Minister of the Interior (1931-32) in the N. Iorga government

Minister of Industry and Trade (1938) and royal counselor (1938)

Prime Minister (1939)

Baciu, Aurel (1886-1953)

Lawyer

Member of the National Christian Party

High ranking official in the Goga government

Bădulescu, Victor (1892-Dec. 1953 or Jan. 1954, Cell number 75)

Lawyer

Professor at the Law Faculty in Bucharest

Prominent member of the National Liberal Party
Director of the Credit Bank
State Secretary at the Ministry of Finance (1935)
Under-Secretary at the Ministry of Foreign Affairs (1936)

Bocu, Sever (1875-1950/51?)

Graduate of the Commercial Academy (Bucharest) and Hautes Etudes School (Paris)
Prominent Member of the National Party and of the National Peasant Party
MP in many Legislatures
Minister in the Maniu government (1928-30), representing the Banat province

Bornemisa, Sebastian (1890-1953)

Writer, Journalist
Ph.D. in Literature (Budapest)
MP representing the National Party (1919-20)
MP representing the Peoples Party (1926-27)
Under-Secretary of State (1938) in the Goga-Cuza government
President of the Romanian Press Union in Ardeal and Banat

Brătianu, Constantin I.C. (Dinu) (1866-Aug. 23, 1953)

Engineer, second son of Ion C. Brătianu
MP from 1895 on
Finance Minister (1933-34)
President of the National Liberal Party
State Minister in the August 23, 1944 government

Brătianu, Gheorghe I. (1898-April 24-25, 1953 Cell number 73)

Son of Ion I.C. Brătianu
Graduate of Law (Iaşi), Literature (Paris); Ph.D. in Philosophy (Cernăuţi), Ph.D. in Literature (Paris)
Professor at the Faculty of Letters in Bucharest

MP

President of the National Liberal Party (Gh. Brătianu wing) (1930-38)

Burilleanu, Dumitru (Tilică) (1878-April 24, 1954)

Governor of the National Bank

Cămărășescu, Ion (Jean) (1882-1953)

Graduate of Law (Paris)

Cabinet Chief at Ministry of Education and Culture

President of the Union of Agricultural Chambers

Minister of the Interior in the Take Ionescu government (1921-22)

Member of the National Peasant Party and MP representing Durostor county in 1919-33

President of the Romanian Delegation to the Economic Council of the "Little Entente" (1934)

Christu, Ion Șerban (1895-1953)

Diplomat

Ph.D. in Law (Paris)

Member of the Economic Division at the Ministry of Foreign Affairs (1928)

Director of the Economic Service at the Ministry of Foreign Affairs (1933)

Plenipotentiary Minister second class (1934)

State Secretary (Feb. 1940)

Minister of Foreign Trade (Feb. 1940)

Director of the Economic Direction at the Ministry of Foreign Affairs (June 1940)

Decorations: Great Officer of the Romanian Crown, The Carol I Commemorative Medal (1939)

Cihoski, Henri (1871-1950)

General of the Army Corps

Minister of War (1928-30) in the Maniu government

Honorary Senator of Parliament

Ciugureanu, Daniel (1885-1950)

Physician
Minister of Basarabia (1918-1919)

Constantinescu, Tancred (1876-1951)

Engineer
Member of the National Liberal Party
MP and Senator in many legislatures
General Director of the Railways
General Secretary at the Ministry of Industry and Trade
Minister of Industry and Trade (1923-26)

Dumitrescu, Grigore (Dorel) (? – June of 1955)

Professor in Roman Law at the Law Faculty of Bucharest
Prominent Member of the National Liberal Party
MP
Governor of the National Bank

Frenţiu, Traian Valeriu (1875-July 11, 1952)

Greek Catholic Bishop of Lugoj and Oradea
Metropolitan Deputy of Blaj

Georgescu, Grigore (1886-1952)

General

Ghiţescu, Stan (1888-1951)

Politician
MP
Vice President of the Deputy Chamber (1926)
Minister of Cooperation (1937-38) under the O. Goga government
Minister of Labor (1940) in the Ion Gigurtu government

Glatz, Alexandru (1882-1953)

General

General Secretary in the Ministry of National Defense

Under-Secretary of State at the Ministry of National Defense (1937; 1939) in the Gh. Tătărăscu and Miron Cristea governments

Ilcuş, Ioan

General

Head of the General Staff

Minister of National Defense (1939;1940) under the C. Argetoianu and Gh. Tătărăscu governments

Lapedatu, Alexandru (1876-1950)

Graduate of History and Geography

Specialist in Medieval History

Professor at Cluj University

President of the Romanian Academy (1935-37)

General Secretary of the Romanian Academy (1937-48)

Co-Director of the Institute of National History

Counselor of the Romanian delegation to the Peace conference in Paris (1918-20) and Geneva (1922)

Member of the National Liberal Party

Senator, 1919-1940, Honorary Senator from March of 1936 on

Minister of Culture and Arts (1923-26, 1928, 1934)

State Minister (1933-34, 1936-37)

Arrested at the age of 75, he died on August 30, 1950
– on St. Alexander's Day

Lapedatu, Ion I. (1876-1950?)

Specialist in Finance, Graduate of the Superior Commercial Academy in Budapest

Professor at the Commercial Academy in Cluj

MP in many legislatures

Senator

Minister of Finance (1926-27) during the Averescu government

Macovei, Ion (1885-Sept. 10, 1950, Cell number 54)

Engineer
General Director of the Railroads
Minister of Public Works (1940)

Maniu, Iuliu (1873-Feb. 5, 1953)

Statesman
Graduate of Law (Cluj, Vienna, Budapest)
Ph.D. in Law (1896)
President of the Directory Council
President of the National Peasant Party
Prime minister (1928-30, 1932-33)
Arrested at 70, he was sentenced to 154 years hard labor
All his life he was faithful to the oath he made as a representative of students: "I swear before God, on my conscience and honor that I will sacrifice my life for the triumph of the Romanian ideal"

Manoilescu, Mihail (1891-Dec. 30-31, 1950, Cell number 67)

Engineer, Graduate of the School for Road and Bridge Construction (Bucharest)
Professor of Economics at the Polytechnic School in Bucharest
Founder of the National Corporate League (1933)
Under-Secretary of State at the Ministry of Finance (1926-27) in the Averescu government
Minister of Communications and Public Works (1930)
Minister of Industry and Trade (1930-31)
Governor of the National Bank (1931)
MP in many Legislatures
Senator
President of the Romanian Section of the International Chamber of Commerce
Foreign Minister (1940)
Purged from the academic life in 1947

Manolescu-Strunga, Ion M. (1889-1951)

Graduate of Vienna University, Ph.D. in Economics (Berlin)

Member of the National Liberal Party

Under-Secretary of State at the Ministry of Agriculture and Domains (1933;1934;1936) under I.Gh. Duca, Dr. C. Angelescu, and Gh. Tătărăscu governments

State Secretary (1937) in the Gh. Tătărăscu government

Măgureanu, Mihail (1886-1951)

Under-Secretary of State to the Prime minister's office (1939) in the Miron Cristea and C. Argetoianu governments

Moşoiu, Tiberiu (1898-?)

Ph.D. in Law (Brussels)

Professor of Roman Law at the Law Faculty in Cluj

Under-Secretary of State at the Ministry of Culture

Under-Secretary of State at the Ministry of Justice and the Ministry of Agriculture and Domains (1937) in the Gh. Tătărăscu government

Governor of the National Bank (1946)

Munteanu-Râmnic, Dumitru (1877-1955)

M.A. in History (Bucharest), History Studies in Paris

Vice-President of the National Democratic Party under the Presidency of N. Iorga

MP (1920 and 1931)

Senator

Secretary of the Federation of Political Parties (1919)

Secretary of the first Chamber of Great Romania (1919)

Under-Secretary of State at the Ministry of the Interior (1931-32) in the Iorga government

Păiş, Nicolae (1886-Aug. 20, 1952 Cell number 27)

Admiral

Graduate of the Superior School of Artillery (Italy) and the Superior

School of War (Paris)
Royal Adjutant (1926-31)
Head of the Navy headquarters (1933)
Under-Secretary of State of the Navy (1940)

Pelivan, Ioan Gh. (1876-Jan 24, 1954)

Graduate of Law and Theology
Professor
Romanian Representative at the Peace Conference in Paris
(1919-1920) and at the Conference in Geneva (1922)
Foreign Minister (1918)
Minister of Justice (1920)
Member of the National Peasant Party
MP in many legislatures
Minister of Basarabia

Pop, Ion (Enci) (1902-1953)

Popovici, Dori (1873-1950)

Minister

Popovici-Epure

General

Popovici-Taşcă, Albert (1881-1951)

Politician
Graduate of Law (Bucharest) Ph.D. in Law (Paris)
Member of Parliament
Under-Secretary of State in the Averescu government

Portocală, Radu (1888-1952)

Lawyer
Lifetime Dean of the Brăila Bar Association

President of the National Liberal Party in Brăila County

Member of Parliament in many legislatures

Under-Secretary of State at the Ministry of the Interior (1936-37)

Knight of the Legion of Honor (France)

Decorated with the royal order of King George I (Greece), the crown order (Italy)

President of the Reșița plants

Potârcă, Virgil (1888-May 10, 1954, Cell number 52)

Graduate of the Faculty of Letters in Paris

Lawyer

President of the Union of the Romanian Agricultural Chamber

Member of the National Peasant Party

Deputy and Senator in all the legislatures since 1920

Under-Secretary of State at the Ministry of Agriculture (1931)

Minister of Justice (1932), Minister of Communications (1937-38) and Ad Interim Minister of Agriculture and Domains (1938)

Racoviță, Mihai-Cehanu (1889-1954)

General of the Army Corps

Minister of National Defense (Aug. 23, 1944)

Racoviță, Mihail I. (1868-July of 1954)

General

Commander and General Inspector of Police

Member of the Agrarian Party

Deputy of Putna and Ismail

Rășcanu, Ioan (1874-1952)

Division General

Military Attaché to Berlin (1907-1911)

Attaché to the French Military Commander (1916)

Brigade Commander in the Mărășești battle

Member of the National Liberal Party

Deputy in many legislatures
Senator
Minister of War (1918-1921)
Minister of Basarabia and Bucovina (1927)
Minister of State (1931-32)
High Commissioner of the government in Basarabia and Bucovina, with rank of Minister (1931)

Roșculeț, Radu (1895-1951)

Graduate of Law at the University of Bucharest
Lawyer
Prefect
Member of the National Liberal Party
Deputy
Minister (1946)

Samsonovici, Nicolae (1877-Sept. 16, 1950)

General
Veteran of the battle of Mărășești (1917)
Chief of Staff under general Ieremia Grigorescu's command
Commander of the Military School (1921)
Head of the General Staff (1928)
War Minister (1932-33), Minister of Industry and Trade (1933)

Sandu, Ion (?-April 1955)

Delegate for Economic issues to the Conference of Peace in Paris (1919)
Deputy Minister (1946)

Simian, Dinu (1887-July 4-5, 1955)

Graduate of Law; Ph.D. in Paris
Lawyer
Member of the National Peasant Party
Deputy (1933)

Vice-President of the Deputy Chamber
Under-Secretary of State in the Ministry of the Interior (1937)
Royal representative for Nistru Region (1938-39) and Olt Region (1939)

Suciu, Ioan (1907-May 27, 1953, Cell 44)

Ph.D. in Rome
At 33 was consecrated Bishop of Oradea
Apostolic Administrator of the Metropolitan Church in Blaj
remarkable orator, surnamed "shepherd of the youth"

Tașcă, Gheorghe (1879-1951)

Graduate of Law; Ph.D. in Economics (Paris)
Lawyer
Professor of Political Economy at the Commercial Academy in
Bucharest
Deputy of the National Peasant Party and Member of the permanent
delegation of this party
Plenipotentiary Minister to Berlin (1930)
Minister of Industry and Trade (1932)

Tătăranu, Constantin (Costel) (1893-Oct. 1953, Cell 12)

Member of the National Liberal Party
Deputy
Governor of the National Bank

Tătărăscu, Alexandru (1888-1951)

General

Vasiliu, Gheorghe (George) (1892-Sept. 10, 1954, Cell 81)

General of Aviation
Under-Secretary of State at the Ministry of Aviation in the Sănătescu
and the Rădescu governments (1944-45)

Vlad, Aurel (1875-1953)

Politician

Ph.D. in Law in Budapest

Head of the Finance department in the Directory Council of Transylvania (1918-20)

Member of the National Peasant Party

Deputy in many legislatures

Minister of Finance in the Vaida government (1919-20)

Minister of Culture (1928-29) Minister of Industry and Trade (1927-30) in the Maniu government

APPENDIX 2

THE LIST OF DIGNITARIES WHO WERE IMPRISONED IN SIGHET BETWEEN MAY 6, 1950 AND JULY 5, 1955

Alimănişteanu, Dimitrie (Dimitru) (1898-?)

Engineer, graduate of the National School of Mining in Paris
Prominent member of the National Liberal Party
Deputy (1933)
Under-Secretary of State at the Ministry of Finance

Angelescu, Constantin (1869-?)

MD, Graduate of the Faculty of Medicine in Paris
Professor at the Faculty of Medicine in Bucharest
Prominent member of the National Liberal Party
Honorary Senator
Minister of Education and Culture
Prime-Minister (1933-34)
Minister of State (1938)
Counselor to the Crown (1938)

Băran, Coriolan (1896-?)

Studies in Budapest and Cluj
Ph.D. in Law
Lawyer
Deputy of the National Peasant Party
Under-Secretary of State at the Ministry of the Interior (1939)

Bejan, Petre P.

Engineer

Deputy in many legislatures
Under-Secretary of State for armaments at the Ministry of War (1935-37)
Under-Secretary of State to the Prime minister's office (1937)
Minister of Industry and Trade (1945-46)

Bentoiu, Aurelian (1892-1962)

Graduate of the Faculty of law in Bucharest
Famous Lawyer
Legislative reporter on the law of conversion of agricultural debts and the law for the defense of order in state
Legislative reporter during the Parliamentary process of the Skoda investigation
Member of the National Liberal Party
Deputy (1933-37)
Under-Secretary of State at the Ministry of Justice (1935;1936-37)
Under-Secretary of State at the Ministry of the Interior (1936 for a few months)
Minister of Justice (1940) during the Tătărăscu government
Was judged in Bucharest between Feb. and June of 1956
Acquitted in June of 1956 and set free from the Văcăreşti prison
Re-arrested in Nov. of 1957, re-judged in spring of 1958 and sentenced to 25 years hard labor
Died on June 27, 1962 in Văcăreşti prison, two days before his seventieth birthday

Berceanu, Mihail G. (1882-?)

Ph.D. in law in Paris
Lawyer
University Professor
Ion I.C. Brătianu's Chief of Cabinet (1909-10)
Deputy
Under-Secretary of State at the Ministry of Domains (1936)
Under-Secretary of State at the Ministry of Industry and Trade (1937)

Bercovitz, Asra (1885-?)

Ph.D. in Philosophy (Paris)
Journalist
Senator of Timiş-Torontal
Member of the National Liberal Party

Berîndă

Uniate Priest (Assumptionist)

Boilă, Zaharia (1892-1955?)

Ph.D. in Law (Budapest)
Journalist
Deputy of the National Peasant Party
Prefect of Tîrnava Mică (1928) and of Hunedoara counties (1932)

Brancovici, Emil Mihail I.

Professor at the Academy for Higher Commercial and Industrial Studies in Bucharest
President of the Union of Cereal Exporters
President of the Union of Urban Proprietors
Deputy (1926)
Senator (1931)

Brătianu, Constantin (Bebe) (1887-?)

Ph.D. in Law (Paris)
General Secretary of the National Liberal Party
Deputy (1922)
General Secretary of the Romanian delegation to the Peace Conference in Paris (1919)
Under-Secretary of State to the Prime minister's office (1927-28)

Brânzeu, Nicolae

Greek-Catholic Canon

Budișteanu, Radu

Well known Lawyer in the Bar Association of Bucharest
Minister of Culture and Arts (1940) in the Ion Gigurtu government

Budurescu, N.

Under-Secretary of State to the Prime minister's office (1933;1934) in the I.Gh. Duca and Gh. Tătărăscu governments

Caracostea, Dumitru (1879-1964)

Graduate of Letters
Ph.D. in Letters and Philosophy
Professor of Romanian Modern Literature at the University of Bucharest
Member of the Romanian Academy
Purged from the University and arrested (1948)

Carandino, Nicolae (1905)

Journalist
Director of The National Theater in Bucharest
Director of the newspaper "Dreptatea", the daily of the National Peasant Party

Cădere, Victor (1891-?)

Ph.D. in Law
Graduate of the School of Political Science (Paris)
Lawyer
Professor in Civil Procedures at The Law Faculty in Cluj
Deputy (1928)
Member of the Romanian delegation at the Peace Conference in Paris (1919-1920)
Chief of Romanian Military Missions in the Far East (Siberia 1920-1921)
Secretary General at the Ministry of Justice (1930)
Secretary General at the Ministry of the Interior (1930-31)
Plenipotentiary Minister to Warsaw and Belgrade

Royal Representative to the Dunărea de Jos Region
Ambassador and Plenipotentiary to Belgrade
Knight of the Romanian Crown with Sword and Ribbon

Cipăianu, Gheorghe (1878-?)

Studies at The Bucharest Academy of Agriculture and at The Agronomic Institute in Leipzig
Ph.D. in Leipzig
Member of the National Liberal Party
Senator
Under-Secretary of State for Agriculture and Domains
Minister of Agriculture and Domains (1934)

Constant, Alexandru

Publicist and Lawyer
Minister of Propaganda (September 1940)
Detained in the Jilava, Aiud, Sighet, Pitești, Rîmnicu Sărat prisons (1946-64)

Cornățeanu, Nicolae D. (1899-1977)

Agronomic Engineer
Ph.D. in Agricultural Sciences (Vienna)
Professor at the Academy for Advanced Agricultural Studies in Bucharest
Minister of Agriculture and Domains (1939) in the Armand Călinescu and Constantin Argetoianu governments

Crețu, Napoleon

Professor of Romanian Language at St. Sava High School in Bucharest
Ministry Under-Secretary of State for Education in the Ion Gigurtu government (1940)
Secretary General at the Ministry of Education (1941)

Cudalbu

Dan, Emanoil

Dan, Sever (1885-?)

Ph.D. in Law and in Political Sciences
Lawyer
Prominent Member of the National Peasant Party
Deputy in many legislatures
Under-Secretary of State for Finances in the Ştirbey government (1927)
Minister of Public Health in the Maniu government
Administrator of the National Bank (1932-1934)

Demetrescu, Camil

M.A., diplomat in Law
Secretary at the Protocol Department, the Ministry of Foreign Affairs (1940)
Deputy director of the Cipher Department at the Ministry of Foreign
Affairs (1943)

Diculescu, Achille (1891-?)

Commander of Aviation
Under-Secretary of State for Aviation (1940)

Dimitriu, Vlad

Member of the Radical Peasant Party

Dragomir, Silviu (1888-1962)

Ph.D. in Theology
Professor of Southeastern European History at the Cluj University
(1923-1947)
Secretary of the Great Assembly in Alba-Iulia (1918)
Deputy (1926-27)
Minister of the Minorities (1939)

Filip, August (1897-?)

Graduate in Law (Paris)
Lawyer
Member of the Agrarian Party
Deputy (1931-32)
Secretary of the Legislative Chamber Commission
Under-Secretary of State to the Prime Minister's Office (1939)

Fotino, George (Gheorghe) (1896-1969)

Ph.D. in Paris
Professor of History of Romanian Law at the Bucharest Faculty of Law
Deputy
Vice-President of the Chamber of Deputies (1934-37)
Minister (1944-45)
Member of the National Liberal Party

Gardone (from Banat)

Georgescu, Ion

Vice-Admiral
Under-Secretary of State for the Navy Department (1944)

Gigurtu, Ion (1886-1959)

Mining Engineer
Graduate of The Academy of Mining in Freiberg and Berlin-Charlottenburg
General Director of the "Mica" Society
Deputy (1926)
Minister of Industry and Commerce (1937-38)
Minister of Public Works and Communications (1939)
Prime minister (1940)

Giurescu, Constantin C. (1901-1977)

Historian

Graduate and Ph.D. in Bucharest; studies in Paris
Professor of Romanian History at the University of Bucharest
Assistant at the Museum of National Antiquities in Bucharest (1920-26)
Member of the Romanian school in France (1923-25)
Director of the Ion C. Brătianu Foundation (1927-30)
Member of the National Liberal Party (Gh. Brătianu)
Deputy in many legislatures
Royal representative to Dunărea de Jos Region (1939)
Minister of the National Renaissance Front (1939-40)
Minister of Propaganda (1940)

Gomoiu, Victor (1882-1960)

Graduate of the Faculty of Medicine in Bucharest; Ph.D. in Medicine (1909)
Surgeon
University Professor, founder of the Romanian Society of Medical History (1929)
President of the World Society of Medical History (1930)
General Secretary at the Ministry of Health (1930)
Minister of Health and Social Welfare (1940)
Cavalier of the Legion of Honor (France 1922)
Died on February 6, 1960 in Aiud prison

Halippa, Pantelimon (Pan) (1883-1979)

Politician, poet, writer
Professor of Theology in Chișinău
Deputy in many legislatures
Minister of State (1919)
Minister of Basarabia (1919-20)
Ad-interim Minister of State of Public Works (1927) in the Barbu Știrbey government
Ad-interim Minister of State of Public Works (1928-30), of Public Works and Communication (1930), Ad-interim Minister of Employment, Health and Social Welfare (1930), Minister of State (1930, 1932-33) in the National Peasant governments

Hațieganu, Emil (1878-?)

Doctor of Law

Professor at the Dept. of Civil Procedure of the Law Faculty in Cluj

President of the National Romanian Council in Cluj (1918)

Deputy (1919, 1926, 1928, 1931)

Vice-President of the Chamber of Deputies

Member of the Directory Council of Transylvania (1918-1920)

Prominent member of the National Peasant Party

Under-Secretary of State of Justice (1930)

Minister of Health, Employment and Social Welfare (1931)

Minister for Transylvania (1932-33)

Member of the "Romanian Front"

Minister in the Petre Groza government (1946) in charge of supervising the electoral process

Hossu, Iuliu (1885-1970)

Studies at the College "De Propaganda Fide" in Rome

Ph.D. in Rome, consecrated bishop of Cluj-Gherla at the age of 32

Member of the delegation which presented King Ferdinand with the document of the Union Transylvania with Romania (1918)

Founding member of the Literary Society ASTRA

Senator

Took active part in the ratification of the concordat with the Greek-Catholic church

Gave a decree to excommunicate all priests who would put themselves to work for the atheist regime

Hudiță, Ion (1896-1982)

Ph.D. in History at Sorbonne

Professor of History of Diplomacy at the University of Bucharest

National Peasant Party Deputy in many legislatures

Minister of Agriculture (1944-45)

Imprisoned between 1947-1955 and 1960-62

Iacobici, Iosif

General
Chief Inspector of the Army
Commander of the 2nd Division of the Mountain Corps
Commander of the 2nd Army Corps
Minister for armaments (1938-39)
Minister of Defense (1941)
Chief of the General Staff of the Operational Troops on the Eastern Front (1941)
Condemned to 8 years of Hard Prison (Jilava, Aiud, Sighet)

Ioaniţescu, D.R. (1885-?)

Politician
Ph.D. in Law (Bucharest)
Professor of Social Politics at the Bucharest Commercial Academy
Minister of Labour, Health and Agriculture in several cabinets
Under-Secretary of State for the Interior (1930)
Member of Parliament in many legislatures
Author of the Law for Police and Gendarmerie
Founder of the Institute of Studies and Education of Workers (1938)

Lazăr, Ilie (1895-1976)

Politician
Graduate of Law, Ph.D. in Cluj, after special studies in economy in Vienna
Deputy (1928-31 and 1932)
Chief of the National Peasant Party of the Maramureş county
Minister Under-Secretary of State

Leon, Gheorghe N. (1888-?)

Graduate of Law (Iaşi)
Ph.D. in Political and Financial Economy (Jena)
Professor of Finances and Statistics at the Law Faculty of Bucharest

President of the Romanian Economists' Association
Member of the National Liberal Party
Deputy
General Secretary and Under-Secretary of State at the Ministry for Commerce and Industry (1934)
Minister of the National Economy (1940-41)

Leucuția, Aurel (Pufi) (1895-?)

Ph.D. graduate of Law (Cluj)
Vice-President of the National Peasant Party of the Timiș-Torontal county
Deputy (1928-30; 1932-33)
Minister of National Economy (1944-45)

Lupaș, Ion (1880-1967)

M.A. in History and Latin (Budapest)
Ph.D. in History
Professor at the University of Cluj
Secretary of the Directory Council of Transylvania (1918-20)
President of the History Section of the Romanian Academy (1932-35)
Member of the National Liberal Party
Deputy
Minister of Health and Social Welfare (1926-27)
Minister of Arts and Culture (1937-38)

Macovei, Victor

Greek-Catholic Canon
Rector of the Blaj Theological Academy

Marinescu, Nicolae

General, M.D.
Minister of Health and Social Welfare (1938-39)
Minister of Health (1944)

Meteș, Ștefan (1887-1977)

Graduate of the Universities of Bucharest and Budapest
Director of the State Archives of Cluj
Deputy (1919-22 and 1931-32)
Under-Secretary of State in the Iorga government (1931-32)

Mihail, Gh.

General
Under-Secretary of State at the Ministry of National Defense (1939)
in the Miron Cristea, Gen. Gh. Argeșanu and C. Argetoianu
governments

Mihalache, Ion (1882-1963)

Schoolmaster
Entered into Politics in 1914; from 1918, distinguished deputy in all
legislatures
Founder of the Peasant Party
Vice-President of the National Peasant Party
Minister of Agriculture and Domains in the Vaida and Maniu
governments (1919-20 and 1928-30)
Minister of the Interior (1930-31 and 1932-33)
Arrested at the age of 65 (1947); was condemned to 104 years forced
labor
Died in prison at Râmnicu Sărat in March of 1963

Mironescu-Mera

Moghioroș

Uniate Bishop

Moldovan, Iuliu (1882-?)

M.D.
Professor of Hygiene and Social Hygiene at the Cluj Medical Faculty
Under-Secretary of State at the Ministry of Labour, Health and Social

Welfare (1930)
Deputy of Hunedoara county
Senator of Arad county

Moldovan, Valer (1875-?)

M.A. in Law (Cluj, Budapest)
Ph.D. in Law (Cluj)
Professor of Administrative Law at the Cluj Law Faculty
Member of the National Peasant Party
Deputy in many legislatures
Senator and Vice-President of the Senate (1928)
Under-Secretary of State for Education and Culture (1928-30) in the Maniu government
General Secretary in the Directory Council of Transylvania (1918-1920)

Moldovan, Victor (1894-?)

Ph.D. in Law
Lawyer
Member of the National Peasant Party
Regional Secretary of the National Peasant Party for Transylvania and Banat
Deputy in many legislatures
Senator and Vice-President of the Senate
Under-Secretary of State at the Ministry of the Interior (1927)

Nicolau, Victor

Niculescu-Buzeşti, Radu (1911-1990)

Engineer
Graduate at The Bucharest Polytechnic

Nistor, Dumitru (1890-?)

Graduate of Theology and Law
Ph.D. in Law (Budapest)

Member of the National Liberal Party
Deputy (1927-28)
Senator (1932)
Chief of the Liberal Organization of the Timiş-Torontal county

Nistor, Ion I. (Iancu) (1876-1962)

M.A. in History (Cernăuți)
Ph.D. in Philosophy (Vienna)
Professor of Romanian History at the University of Cernăuți
Member of the National Liberal Party
Deputy
Senator
Minister of Bucovina (1918-26)
Minister of Basarabia (1919)
Minister of Public Works (1927-28), of Labour, Health and Social Welfare (1935-36), of Arts and Culture (1939-40)

Nițescu, Voicu

Graduate of Law
Politician and Journalist
President of the Romanian National Committee to Russia (1919)
Technical Advisor to the Peace Conference in Paris (1919)
Deputy in many legislatures
Minister of State (1928-30)
Under-Secretary of State at the Ministry of Justice (1930)
Minister of Justice (1930-31)
Minister of Public Works and Communications (1930), of Agriculture and Domains (1933)
Minister of Labor (1938)

Papacostea, Victor (1900-1962)

Ph.D. in Literature and Philosophy (Bucharest)
Professor at the University of Bucharest
Founder and director of: The Institute for Balkan Studies

(1938-1947); Director of the "Balcania" review
Member of the National Liberal Party (Gh. Brătianu)
Deputy of Caliacra (1932)
Ministry Under-Secretary of State for National Education (1944-45)
Purged from the University in 1947
Re-arrested in the period of 1956-57 (the process of A. Bentoiu).
Freed from lack of evidence.

Pacha, Augustin

Catholic Bishop of the Timişoara Diocese

Pătrăşcanu, Lucreţiu (1900-1954)

Professor of Constitutional Law at the University of Bucharest
Minister of Justice (August 23, 1944 – 1948)
A leader of the Romanian Communist Party
Overturned the Law of life-time tenancy for Magistrates
Executed by his communist rivals after a mock trial (1954)

Păun

Pâclişanu, Zenobie (1886-?)

Studies in Theology in Vienna
Prelate, journalist
Professor of Theology in Blaj
Secretary of the Grand Assembly at Alba Iulia (December 1, 1918)
Director in the Ministry of Culture
Vicar of Bucharest

Penescu, Nicolae

Ph.D. in Juridical Science at the University of Paris
Lawyer
President of the Lawyers Union of Romania
General Secretary of the National Peasant Party
Was imprisoned between 1947-1964

Periețeanu, I. Gr. (Ionel)

Graduate of Law
Lawyer and Poet
Inspector of the Bucharest Police
Deputy of the Ilfov county in many legislatures
Vice-President of the Assembly of Deputies (1930-31)
Member of the National Peasant Party
Minister of Communications in the Vaida-Voevod cabinet (1932)
Joined the "Romanian Front"
President of the Lawyers Union of Romania (1935 and 1938)
Vice-President of the International Union of Lawyers
Vice-President of the Senate

Petrescu, Ion C.

Lecturer on the History of Pedagogy at the University of Bucharest
Member of the National Peasant Party
Under-Secretary of State for Cults (1941-44)

Pop, Romulus G.

M.A. in Law; studies in Geneva, Grenoble and Paris
Ph.D. in Law
Member of the National Peasant Party
Deputy (1932-33)

Popescu-Necșești, Al.

M.A. in Literature, Philosophy and Law (Bucharest)
Lawyer and Journalist
Member of the National Liberal Party
Deputy of the Hotin county
General Secretary at the Ministry of Justice (1927)
Member of the High Council of State Attorneys
Under-Secretary of State at the Ministry of Education and Cults
(1933-34)

Popovici, Mihai (1879-1956?)

Politician
M.A. in Philosophy (Vienna)
Ph.D. in Law
Member of the National Peasant Party
Member of the Directory Council of Transylvania (1918-1920), at the Department of Industry and Commerce
Minister of Public Works and ad-interim of Finances (1919-20)
Minister of Finances (1927, 1929, 1930-31), of the Interior (1930) and of Justice (1932-33)

Priboianu, Mihail M.

Engineer
Graduate of the National School of Mining in Paris
President of the National Peasant Party Organization in the Durostor county
Prefect (1929-30)
Deputy (1928-31; 1932-33)
Minister for armaments (1940)

Rădulescu-Pogoneanu, Victor (Piki) (1910-?)

Career Diplomat
Graduate in Law, Philosophy and Literature (Bucharest)
Legation Attaché (1934)
Class III Secretary at Romanian Legation in Berlin (1937)
Class II Secretary (1941)

Romaşcanu, Mihail

Romniceanu, Mihail M. (1891-?)

Law Graduate
Lawyer
Professor at the Faculty of Law in Bucharest
Executive Committee Member of the National Liberal Party (1932)

Senator of the Hunedoara county (1933)

Reporter on the Debt Conversion law for the new statutes of the National Bank

Minister (1946) in charge of supervising correct electoral processes during the Petre Groza government

Russu, Alexandru (1884-1963)

Studies in Theology in Budapest

Greek-Catholic Bishop at the Baia Mare Diocese

Professor at the Theological Academy in Blaj

Dies in 1963 and is buried in a detainees cemetery in Gherla with only a sign over his grave reading "number 133"

Russu

Greek-Catholic Priest

Secretary to Ion Suciu, Head of Metropolitan Uniate church in Blaj

Sassu, Vasile (1878-1976)

Politician

Graduate of Law and Philosophy (Bucharest)

Member of the National Liberal Party

Deputy in the Vaslui county (1907-1910)

Minister of Commerce and Industry (1922-23; and 1934), of Agriculture and Domains (1937) and of Justice

Sălăjan

Greek-Catholic Priest

Sauciuc-Săveanu, Teofil (1884-1971)

Graduate in Philosophy (Vienna and Cernăuți)

Ph.D. in Literature and Philosophy

Professor of Classic Philology at the University of Cernăuți

Professor of Ancient History and Epigraphy at the Faculty of Letters in Bucharest

Deputy

Member of the permanent delegation of the National Peasant Party
Senator
Minister of State (1928-29; 1932-33)
Director of the Ministry of Cernăuți (1930-31)

Sibiceanu, Nicolae

Cabinet Director of prime minister Gh. Tătărăscu
Under-Secretary of State to the Prime Minister (1939-1940)
Under-Secretary of State at the Ministry of Arts and Culture (1940)

Slăvescu, Victor I. (1891-1977)

Ph.D. in Finance and Economics (Halle)
Professor at the Commercial Academy in Bucharest
General Director of the National Society for Industrial Credit
Member of the National Liberal Party
Deputy in many legislatures
Under-Secretary of State (1933-34)
Minister of Finances (1934-35)
Under-Secretary of State for Armaments (1939)

Solomon, Virgil

Member of the National Liberal Party
Minister

Sova

General

Strat, Gheorghe Z. (1894-1961)

Graduate of Law (Iași)
Ph.D. in Law (Paris)
Professor of the History of Economic Doctrines at the Bucharest Law
Faculty
Veteran of the Oituz and Mărășești battles (1917)
Decorated with the Romanian Crown

Member of the National Liberal Party

Deputy in many legislatures

Representative for Romania to the League of Nations in Geneva (1938)

Founded the Academy of Moral and Political Sciences and was it's secretary

Under-Secretary of State at the Ministry of National Economy (1940)

Editor-in-chief of the newspaper "Libertatea" (1940)

Purged from the University in 1947

Re-arrested with the Bentoiu group (1956-57); condemned to 25 years

Detained in the prisons of Jilava, Galaţi, and Botoşani where he died in 1961

Ştefănescu-Goangă, Florian (1881-?)

Graduate of Law and Philosophy

Professor of Psychology at the University of Cluj

Director and Founder of the first Institute of Experimental Psychology (1921)

Under-Secretary of State for Education (1936)

Tătărăscu, Emanuel N. (1892-?)

Director of the Anonymous Society "Scrisul Românesc" in Craiova

Member of the National Liberal Party

Mayor

Deputy (1933)

Tătărăscu, Gheorghe (1886-1957)

Politician and Publicist

Ph.D. in Law (Paris)

Under-Secretary of State at the Ministry of the Interior (1923-28)

General Secretary of the National Liberal Party (1931)

Minister of Commerce and Industry in the Duca and C. Angelescu governments

Prime-Minister (1934-37)

Minister of State and ad-interim for Foreign Affairs (1938)

Ambassador to Paris

Ad-interim Minister of the Interior (1939)
Prime-Minister (1939-1940)
Vice-President of the Council of Ministers and the Ministry of
Foreign Affairs (1945-47)

Tătărăscu, Ştefan

Teodorescu (Malacul)

Tomescu, Constantin N.

M.A. and Ph.D. in Theology (Bucharest)
Professor of the History of Romanian Churches at the Faculty of
Theology in Chişinău
General Secretary of Churches in Basarabia
Deputy
Minister in the Octavian Goga government (1938)

Ţoni, D.V. (1885-1955?)

Publicist
Deputy in many legislatures
Under-Secretary of State for National Education

Vântu, Gheorghe G. (1894-1968)

Graduate of Law
Member of the National Liberal Party
Prefect of Cernăuţi (1940)
Under-Secretary of State at the Ministry of the Interior (1940) in the
Gh. Tătărăscu government
Under-Secretary of State at the Ministry of the Interior (1946)

Vultur, Ion

Greek-Catholic Priest
Professor of French at the Theological Academy in Blaj

Zamfirescu, Constantin Căteasa

Member of the National Liberal Party
Deputy in many legislatures
Minister in the Sănătescu government (1944)
Under-Secretary of State (1944-45) in the Rădescu government

Zigre, Nicolae

Ph.D. in Law
Lawyer
Vice-President of the Lawyers Union of Romania
Member of the National Liberal Party (Gh. Brătianu)
Prefect of Bihor county in many legislatures
Senator
Vice-President of the Senate (1927-28)
Under-Secretary of State at the Ministry of the Interior
Minister of Arts and Culture (1939)

Zwiedenek, Anton

General
Marshall of the Palace

APPENDIX 3

NAMES OF SIGHET DETAINEES NOT INCLUDED IN APPENDIXES 1 AND 2

The communist penitentiary system was based on utmost secrecy.

Any attempt to communicate, to get information about what went on in prisons, was repressed with cruelty.

Therefore, we considered it necessary to compile this list in order to complete – as much as possible – the list of those who suffered in Sighet Penitentiary. Of course, this list is still open.

We found these names as well as some data from the following sources: Creangă, Mihai – *Sighet's Reputation is Changing* in *Cotidianul*, year III, no.121 (553), Wednesday May 26, 1993; *Dreptatea*, year XXII, (no. 259) Wednesday Dec. 12, 1990, see page 1– the list of those who died in the prison of Sighetul Marmației during four years, eight months and six days, between May 5, 1950 and Feb. 6, 1955); Ionițoiu, Cicerone – *The Golden Book of the Romanian resistance against Communism*; Roșca, Nuțu Dr. – *The Ministers' Prison* in *The Sighet prison accuses, 1950-55*, Gutinul S.R.L. publishers, Baia Mare, 1991; Mușat, Mircea and Ardeleanu, Ion – *Romania after the Great Union*, Scientific and Encyclopedic Publishing House, Bucharest, 1988; *C.I.C. Brătianu, Carol II, Ion Antonescu. Memories. Documents. Correspondence* – Published by Ion Ardeleanu, Forum S.R.L. Publishing House, Bucharest 1992.

Lia Ioana Ciplea

Dinu C. Giurescu

Angelescu, Constantin (1883-?)

M.A. at the Bucharest Faculty of Law
Member of the "Romanian Front"
Deputy in many legislatures
Senator
Under-Secretary of State at the Ministry of the Interior
Governor of the National Bank
Vice-President of the Chamber of Deputies
Minister of the National Economy (1940) in the Gh. Tătărăscu
government

Antonescu, Ervin

Professor of Law at the Bucharest Commercial Academy
Died in Sighet prison

Bălan, Ion (1880-1959)

Studies in Blaj and Budapest
Professor at Theological Academy in Blaj (1920)
Bishop of Lugoj
Arrested in 1948
Imprisoned in Sighet from 1950-55

Berinde, Ştefan

Uniate Priest

Bideanu, Augustin

Under-Secretary of State at the Ministry of Finance (1940) in the Ion
Gigurtu government

Boga, Alniziu (Aloiziu) (1886-1954)

Died in prison in Sighet

Bujoiu, Ion

Engineer
Minister of Industry and Commerce (1937) in the Gh. Tătărăscu government
Minister of National Economy (1939) in the Miron Cristea government

Chertes, Ion

Consecrated secretly as bishop
In the Sighet prison, 1948-1955
Re-arrested in 1956 and condemned to forced labor for life
Was also in the Aiud and Gherla prisons
Pardoned in 1964

Chinezu, Tit-Liviu (?-May 15, 1955)

Studies in Rome
Professor of Philosophy at the Theological Academy in Blaj (1930-1946)
Arrested in 1948
Consecrated as bishop secretly by Bishop Traian Valeriu Frenţiu
Died in Sighet penitentiary

Deliman, Ion

Archpriest
Arrested in 1948

Dobrescu, Aurel R. (1885-?)

Medical studies in Graz, Geneva, Vienna and Bucharest
National Peasant Party member
Deputy in many legislatures
Senator
Under-Secretary of State for Agriculture and Domains (1928)

Durcovici, Anton (?-1951)

Catholic Bishop of Iași

Arrested in 1949, detained at the Ministry of the Interior, in Gherla and Sighet, where he died

Finţescu, Ion N. (1888-?)

Professor of Commercial Law at the Bucharest Law Faculty

Dean of the Faculty of Law

General Administrator of the National Industrial Credit

Member of the National Liberal Party

Deputy

Minister of the National Economy (1942-44)

Was imprisoned at Jilava, Aiud and Sighet

Friedrich, Rafael

Roman-Catholic Canon

Professor of Theology in Iași

Imprisoned between 1949-1962 in Sighet (Cell 44), Gherla....

Grigorovici, Gheorghe (1871-February 1951)

Medical studies in Vienna

President of the Social Democrat Party of Austria

Deputy in the Austrian Parliament (1907-1918)

Member of the National Council of Bucovina (1918)

Editor and Director, in Cernăuţi, of the Social-Democrat newspapers "Lupta" (the Fight) and "Vremea Nouă" (New Times)

Deputy and Senator (1919-1921)

Under-Secretary of State at the Ministry of Labour (Nov. 1939 – May 1940) in the Gh. Tătărăscu government

Died in prison in Sighet

Gruia, Ion V. (1895-1952)

M.A. in Law (Iași)

Ph.D. (Bucharest)

Lawyer

Professor of Constitutional and Administrative Law at the University of Bucharest

Member of the Royal Institute of Administrative Sciences of Romania

Deputy

Minister of Justice (1940) in the Ion Gigurtu government

Arrested in 1949

Died in prison in Sighet

Gruia-Ionescu, Nicolae (1902-1953)

Iliescu, Victor (1884-1959)

General

Distinguished himself in the battle in Răzoare during WW1 (1916)

Decorated with the Romanian Crown and Romanian Star for deeds of bravery in WW1

Under-Secretary of State for National Education (1941-43)

Arrested in 1946; sentenced to 10 years in 1948

Was incarcerated in Aiud, Jilava, Sighet prisons

Freed in 1956

Jienescu, Gheorghe

Commander of Aviation

Under-Secretary of State for the Department of National Defense (1940– August 23, 1944)

Was imprisoned in Aiud, Jilava, Sighet

Died in detention at Râmnicu Sărat

Lugoşianu, Ion (1890-1957)

Graduated from the Faculty of Law and the School of Political Science (Paris)

Lawyer

Member of the National Peasant Party

Deputy

Technical Counselor to the Romanian Delegation at the Peace Conference in Paris (1919)

Cabinet Chief in the Vaida-Voevod government (1919-20)

Commissioner of the Government of Romania in the United States and Canada for the organization of Consulate Services

Close collaborator of Iuliu Maniu

Under-Secretary of State to the Prime Minister (1928-30)

Minister of Education (1930)

Minister of Industry and Commerce (1932; 1933)

Delegate to the League of Nations in Geneva, Paris, the Hague

Director of the newspaper "Universul" (the Universe)

Maghiar, Augustin (1880– September 16, 1951)

Catholic Canon

Arrested in 1948, died in prison in Sighet

Man(u), Demetriu (Dumitru)

Greek-Catholic Canon

Professor at the Cluj Theological Seminary

Member of the National Peasant Party

Deputy

Died in detention

Mareş, Nicolae (1875-1953)

Engineer

Minister of Agriculture and Domains (1940-41)

Died in detention in Sighet

Marton, Aron (1896-1980?)

Catholic Bishop of the Alba-Iulia diocese

In 1949 he expressed public solidarity with the Romanian Greek-Catholic Church, outlawed by a governmental decree (December 1948)

Arrested in 1950, and was imprisoned at Jilava, Aiud and Sighet

Medveczki, Ştefan (1905-1952)

Moldovan, Ion

Canon

Motaş, Constantin I. (1887-?)

Graduate and Ph.D. degrees at the Academy of Mining in Freiburg
Professor at the Institute of Oil and Gas in Bucharest
Member of the Romanian Academy
Prominent member of the Social Democrat Party (Party wing led by Constantin Titel Petrescu)
Deputy of the Tîrnava Mică county (1922-26)
Arrested in 1950; freed in 1956

Nemoianu, Petre (1889-1951?)

Ph.D. in Law and Political Sciences
Lawyer and journalist
Member of the National Christian Party
Prefect of the Caraş Severin county (1920-21)
Deputy (1926-27)
President of the National Christian Party Organization in the Severin county
Under-Secretary of State at the Ministry of Agriculture and Domains (1940) in the Ion Gigurtu government
Arrested and imprisoned in Sighet and Aiud
Died in prison in Aiud

Nicolau, Pompiliu

Engineer
Graduate of the National School of Bridges and Highways in Bucharest
Professor at the Timişoara School of Polytechnics
Minister of Public Works (1941)
Was imprisoned in Jilava, Aiud and Sighet

Ottulescu, Alexandru (1881-?)

Graduate in Law

Lawyer

Attorney at the Ministry of Finances, and Juridical Counselor at the Ministry of Foreign Affairs

Governor of the National Bank from 1941 till 1944 when he resigned

Is believed to have died in Sighet

Pană, Aurelian (?-1953)

Under-Secretary of State at the Ministry of Agriculture (1941-43)

Arrested and imprisoned in Jilava, Sighet and Gherla

Died in detention in Gherla

Petrescu, Constantin-Titel (1888-?)

Graduate of the Paris Faculty of Law

Lawyer

General Secretary of the Federation of Social Democratic Parties (1922-1927)

Minister in the first government presided over by Gen. Constantin Sănătescu (1944)

Ploscaru, Ion

General Vicar of the Lugoj Diocese

Consecrated Bishop secretly (1948) by the Papal Envoy O'Hara

Imprisoned in Sighet between 1950 and 1955

Pop, Valer(iu) (1892-?)

Ph.D. in law (Cluj)

Lawyer

Member of the National Liberal Party

Deputy in many legislatures

Vice-President of the Chamber of Deputies (1931)

Minister of State for Transylvania (1931-32)

Minister of Justice (1934-36)
Minister of Industry and Commerce (1936-37)
Minister Secretary of State (1937) in the Gh. Tătărăscu government

Popa, Eugen

Uniate Priest
Imprisoned in Sighet between 1950 and 1955, in Cell 44
Presently Rector at the Theological Institute in Cluj

Rațiu, Alexandru

Greek-Catholic Priest
Arrested in 1948; was imprisoned for 16 years
Freed in 1964

Rațiu, Iuliu

Archpriest of Timișoara

Răducanu, Ion

Professor at the Commercial Academy in Bucharest
Member of the National Peasant Party
Member of the permanent delegation of the National Peasant Party
Deputy in many legislatures
Minister of Labour and Social Welfare (1928-1930)
Minister of Public Works (1930-31)
Purged from the Academic life in 1947
Arrested in 1950

Sachelarie, Ovidiu (1906-?)

Professor of Civil Law at the Bucharest Law Faculty
Purged from the Academic life in 1948
Arrested, was imprisoned in Jilava, Aiud and Sighet

Scheffler, Ioan

Catholic Bishop of Satu-Mare and Oradea
Arrested in 1949, died in prison in Sighet

Schubert, Iosef

Catholic Bishop, consecrated secretly by Papal Envoy O'Hara (1950)
Arrested in 1951
Condemned to hard labor for life and was imprisoned in Jilava,
Sighet, Oradea, Aiud, Pitești, Dej....

Sichitiu, Ion (?-1952)

General
Chief of the General Staff
Professor at the Military Academy
Member of the "Romanian National Front"
Senator
Minister of Agriculture and Domains (1941-42)
Died in prison in Aiud

Stoenescu, Nicolae

Minister

Strihan, Petre

Lecturer at the Commercial Academy in Bucharest
Under-Secretary of State at the Ministry of the Interior and Territorial
Administration (1942-23 August 1944)
Was imprisoned in Aiud, Jilava and Sighet

Todea, Alexandru

Consecrated Bishop secretly (1950) by the bishop Iosef Schubert
Arrested in 1951, was condemned to hard labor for life
Detained in Aiud, Sighet and Gherla prisons
Freed in 1964

Vezoc, Iosif

Greek-Catholic Canon

Vida, Ludovic

Canon

General Vicar of the Greek-Catholic diocese at Baia Mare

Arrested in 1948

Imprisoned in Sighet for 5 years

Re-arrested in 1957, condemned to 10 years of hard labor, imprisoned in Gherla.

INDEX